The Development of Western Music

An Anthology

Volume II

Second Edition

The Development of Western Music

An Anthology

Volume II

Nineteenth Century,
Twentieth Century

Edited by

K Marie Stolba

*Professor of Music, Emerita
Indiana University–Purdue
University at Fort Wayne*

 **WCB Brown & Benchmark**
PUBLISHERS

Madison, Wisconsin • Dubuque, Iowa

Book Team

Developmental Editor *Deborah D. Reinbold*
Production Editor *Suzanne M. Guinn*
Designer *Lu Ann Schrandt*
Permissions Coordinators *Vicki Krug and LouAnn Wilson*
Visuals/Design Developmental Consultant *Marilyn A. Phelps*
Visuals/Design Freelance Specialist *Mary L. Christianson*
Publishing Services Specialist *Sherry Padden*
Marketing Manager *Steven Yetter*
Advertising Manager *Nancy Milling*

A Division of Wm. C. Brown Communications, Inc.

Executive Vice President/General Manager *Thomas E. Doran*
Vice President/Editor in Chief *Edgar J. Laube*
Vice President/Sales and Marketing *Eric Ziegler*
Director of Production *Vickie Putman Caughron*
Director of Custom and Electronic Publishing *Chris Rogers*

Wm. C. Brown Communications, Inc.

President and Chief Executive Officer *G. Franklin Lewis*
Corporate Senior Vice President and Chief Financial Officer *Robert Chesterman*
Corporate Senior Vice President and President of Manufacturing *Roger Meyer*

Cover illustration by Jay Bryant

Consulting Editor Frederick W. Westphal

S. D. G.

Contents

Modern

Preface to the Second Edition

This second edition of *The Development of Western Music: An Anthology* is a two-volume historical anthology of music specifically designed to present music to be studied in conjunction with the second edition of the text *The Development of Western Music: A History.* With few exceptions, the selections are complete movements or complete compositions. The works are presented in the Anthology in the same order in which they are mentioned or discussed in the History text. Volume I contains selections representative of music from Ancient Times through the Classical Era; Volume II holds compositions characteristic of the transition from Classical to Romantic music, and Romantic and Modern works. Sets of sound recordings of the selections in the Anthology have been prepared and are available in either CD or cassette form for use with the Anthology and the History text. The music is printed in the Anthology in its original key; however, the recording, particularly of vocal music, may be in a different key. The recordings are intended to be a historical presentation; when feasible, recordings using period instruments have been selected. Because tuning was not standardized prior to 1700, there may be some instances in which the recorded music sounds "out of tune" to modern ears.

Texts of vocal music are presented in their original language, with English translation. Most of the translations of poetic and prose texts are my own; the work of other persons is acknowledged. I am indebted to Father Dick John of St. Francis College, Fort Wayne, for assistance with some medieval Latin texts containing particular ecclesiastical expressions, and to Miguel Roig-Francoli for help in translating some Spanish and Galician poetry.

Although this Anthology was designed to complement the History text, the Anthology is complete in itself, and its selections can serve as works for study and analysis in Form and Analysis, Music Literature, Music Theory, or other music courses.

It is impossible to name all those who contributed to this project. From time to time, several of my colleagues, particularly John Loessi and Masson Robertson, have loaned me music from their personal libraries. Jody Smith graciously consented to copy into music calligraphy my transcriptions from manuscripts. Many libraries have shared their holdings with me. Great demands have been made upon the Music Library at Indiana University, Bloomington, and thanks are due especially to Music Librarian R. Michael Fling, and the reference assistants, who responded promptly to my requests for materials. The librarians in the Inter-Library Loan/Document Delivery Services department at Helmke Library, IPFW, were most helpful in procuring materials. Marilyn Grush spent much time helping me research sources at the OCLC station there. I wish to express my gratitude to Kenneth Balthaser, who made available the facilities at the IPFW Learning Resource Center and the services of its technicians in the preparation of camera-ready proof, particularly Roberta Sandy Shadle.

Where no specific modern publication is cited, the music was transcribed and/or edited from original sources. Brown & Benchmark and I are grateful to the persons and publishers who have granted permission to reprint, edit, or adapt material for which they hold copyright. I wish to express my appreciation also to my editors at Brown & Benchmark, who carefully considered my requests, and to my book team and all other persons who were involved in the production of these volumes.

K Marie Stolba
Fort Wayne, Indiana

Free binary
AB-AB form

135. NOCTURNE NO. 5
John Field (1782–1837)

136. ECLOGUE XXXVI, Op. 66, No. 6
Václav Jan Tomášek (1774–1850)

Editio Supraphon, The Czech Republic.

*) Orig. ♩.

*) Orig. ℔   **) Orig. ℔

*) Orig. *f*, anche bat. 66, bat. 68, 69.

- doesn't experiment harmonically
- melody almost always in upper voices
- limited amount of material

· uses same material until ‖

A B A
· Da Capo

Da Capo fin che al Fine

* Sonata allegro form*
reuse of thematic material
developement of ♩
•use one motive.

137. PIANO SONATA NO. 23,
Op. 57, "Appassionata," mvt. 1
Ludwig van Beethoven (1770–1827)

Allegro assai

*) In second part of 1st theme and the following
passages based thereon, the slurs in autogr.
and orig. edition are by no means uniform;
this divergence has been rectified throughout.

*) In autogr. and orig.ed., the slurs in the 2. theme
and its repetitions are also very dissimilar; here too
this disagreement has been corrected throughout.

*) In autograph and orig. edition e^2 instead of fb^2.
**) And also octave $e–e^1$ (above on the contrary fb^3).

development

*) In the autograph and the original edition,
inner voice *Bb* (not *G*).

*) In the autograph and the original edition
the prefix to the trill is lacking; cf. bar 44.

*) *f* only in autograph, not in orig. edition.

1ST movement of symphony: Sonata Allegro
(4 movements) keys: I - V - IV - I
IV - V
1st 2nd 3rd 4th

Concerto (3 movements) 1ST: Sonata Allegro with double exposition

138. SYMPHONY NO. 3 "Eroica," mvt. 1
Ludwig van Beethoven (1770-1827)

Allegro con brio. ♩. = 60.

Flauti.

Oboi.

Clarinetti in B.

Fagotti.

Corni in Es.

Corno 3ᵗᵒ in Es.

Trombe in Es.

Timpani in Es. B.

Violino I.

Violino II.

Viola.

Violoncello e Basso.

1st theme

*much use of
hammer chords*

13

26

Modulatory or Bridge theme

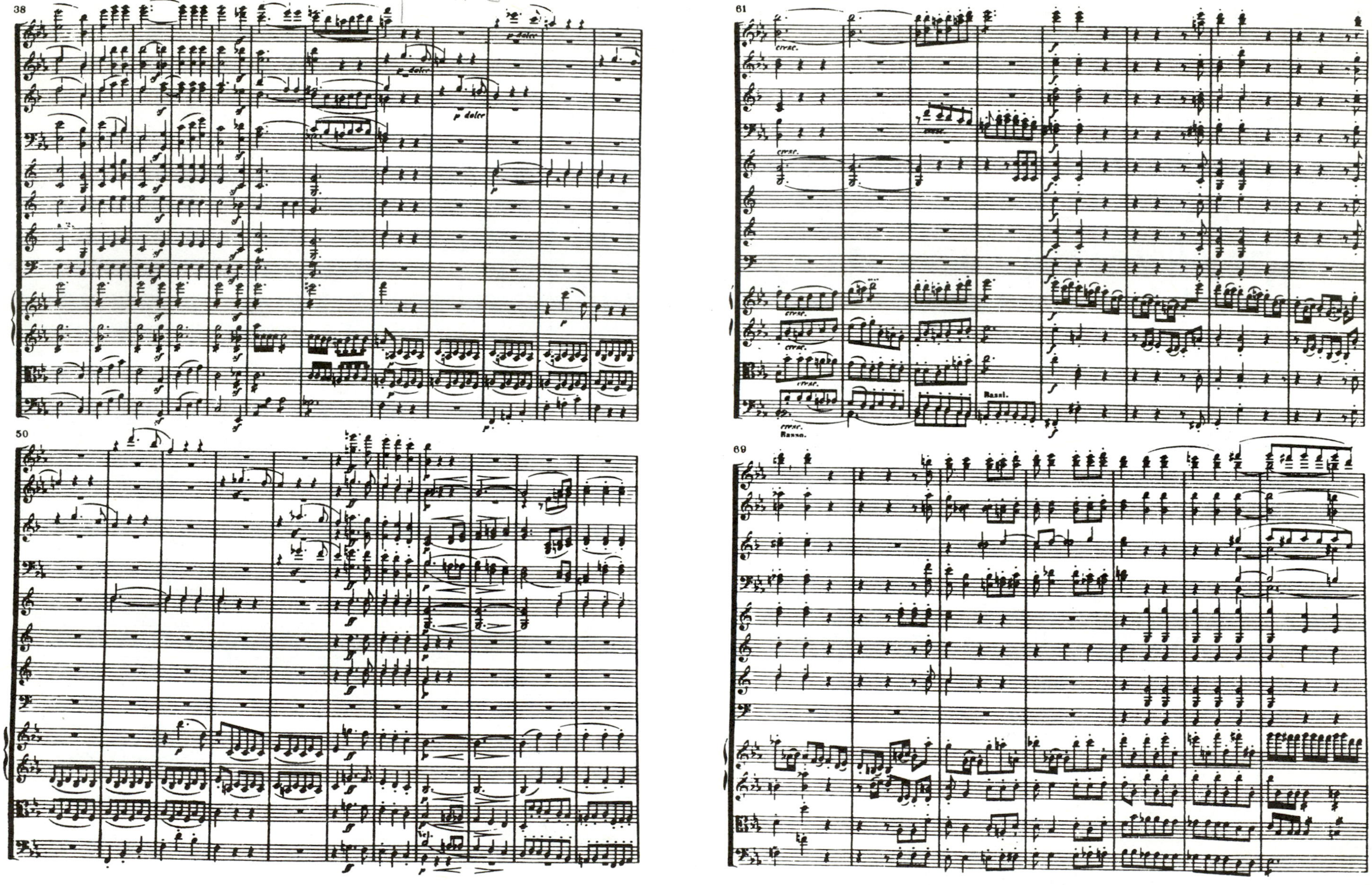

more lyric

2nd strong theme

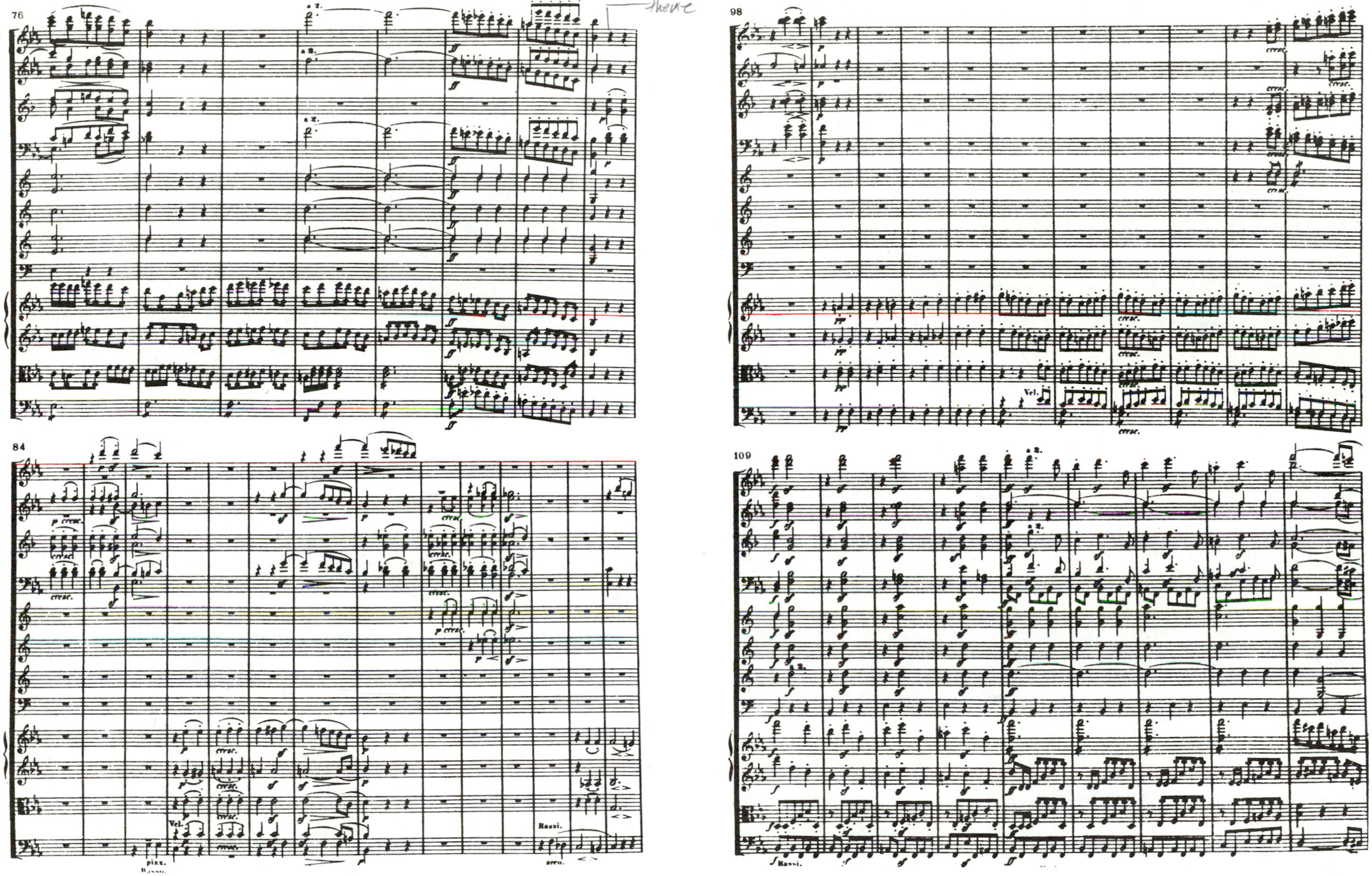

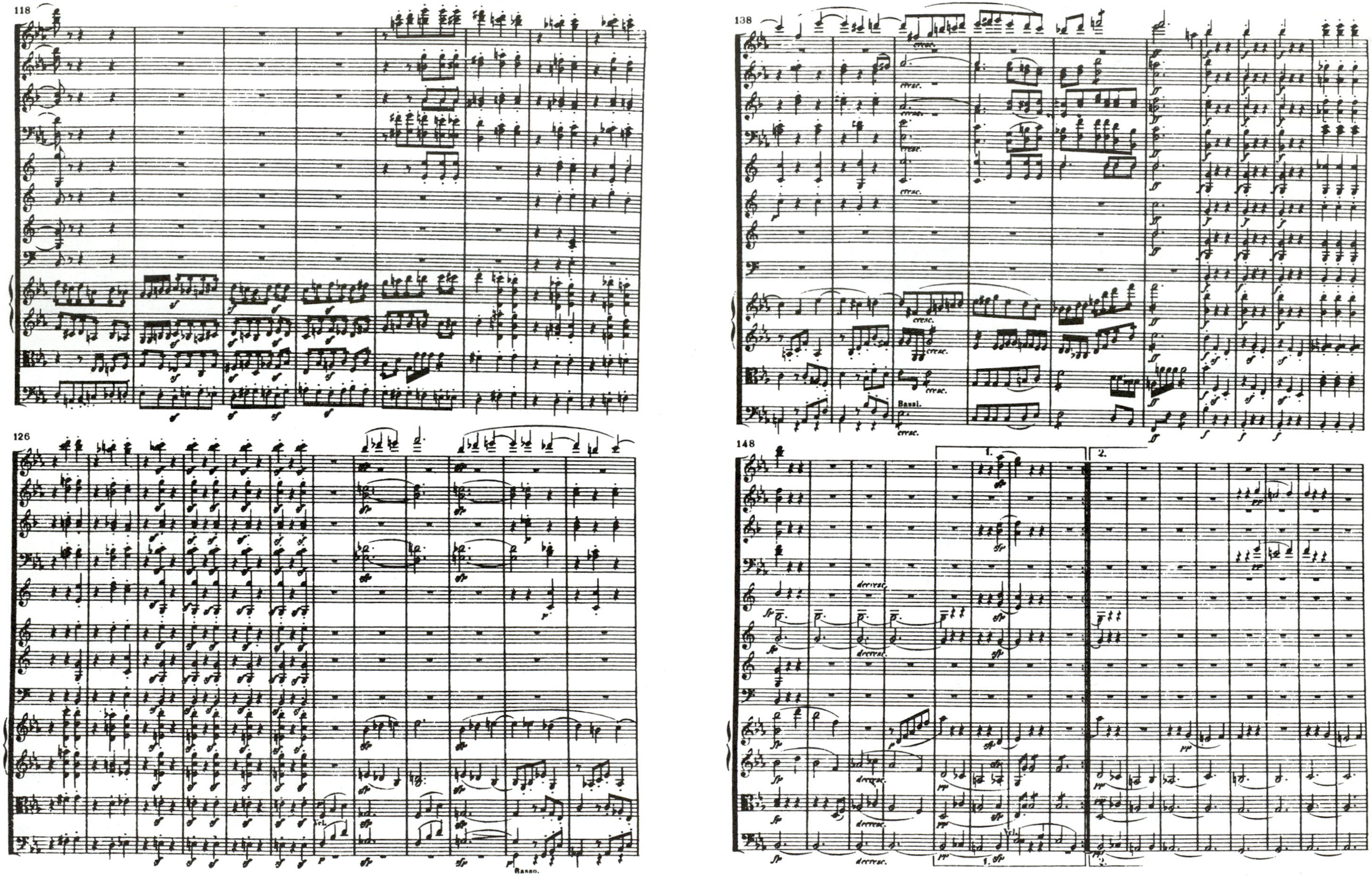

L

1st exposition ends

Developement

← hemiola – 3beats against 2 →

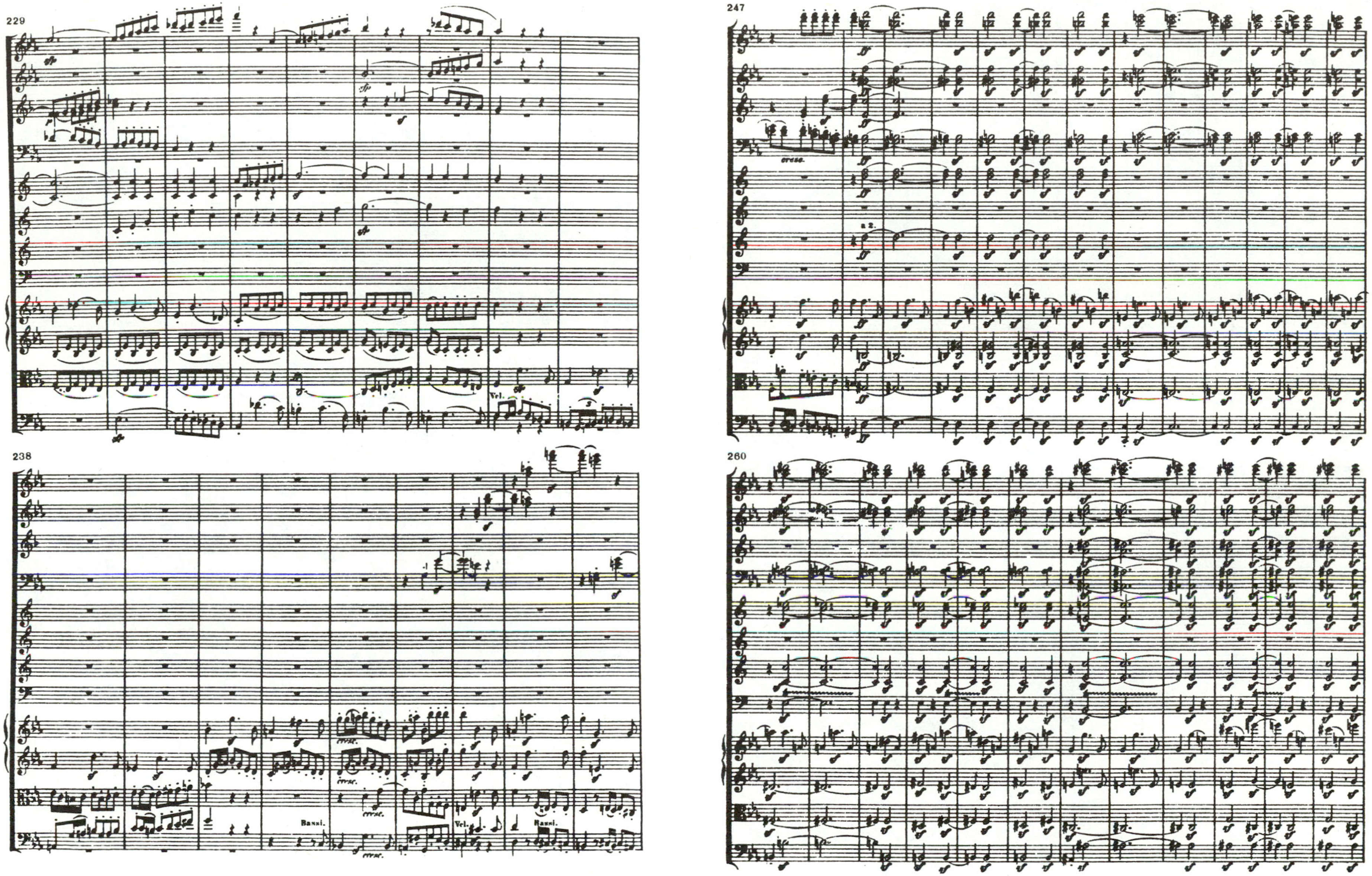

Variation of 1st theme

21

2nd theme

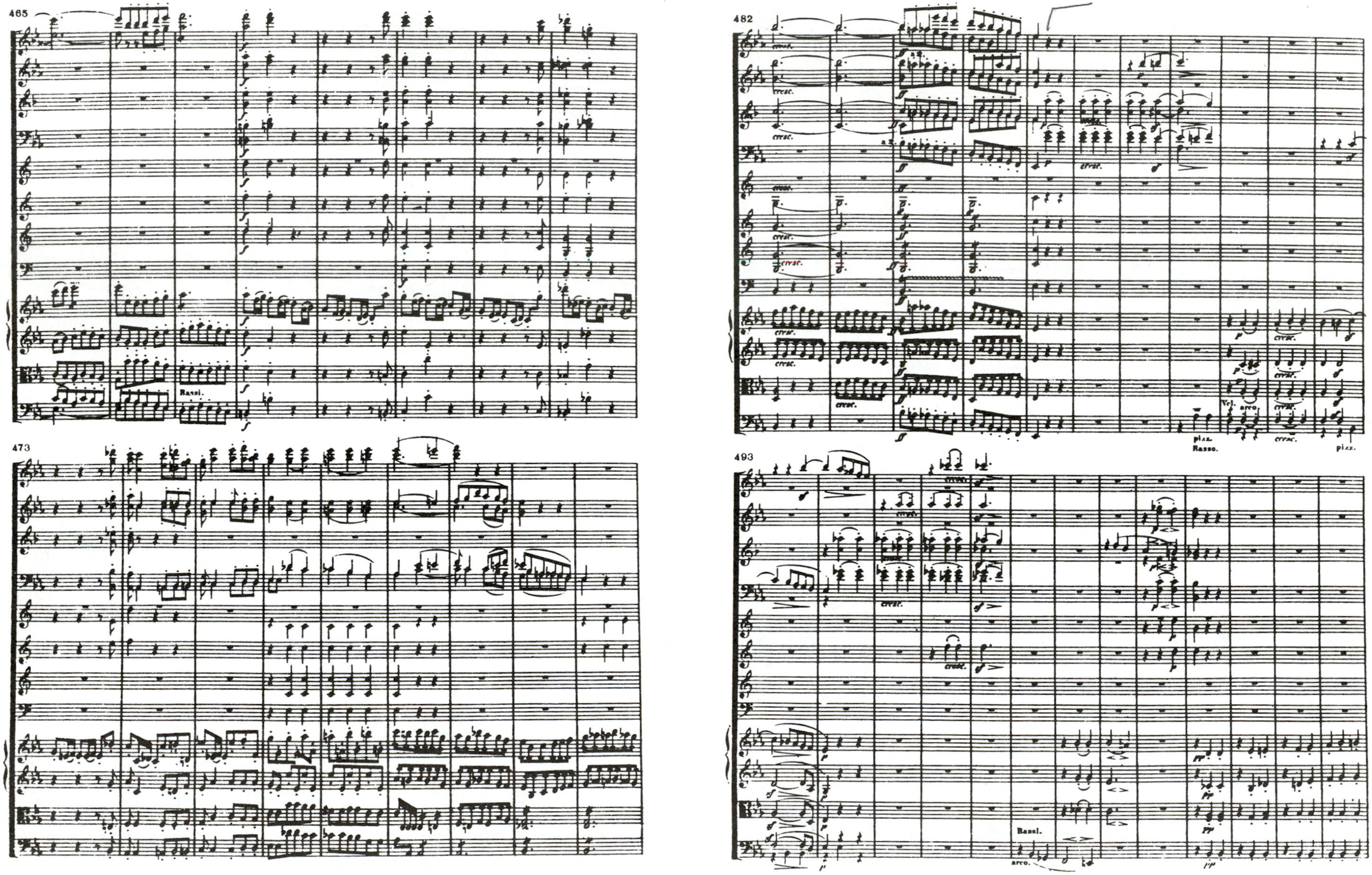
465
Bassi.
473
482
cresc.
a 2.
pizz.
Basso.
Vcl.
arco
493
Bassi.
arco

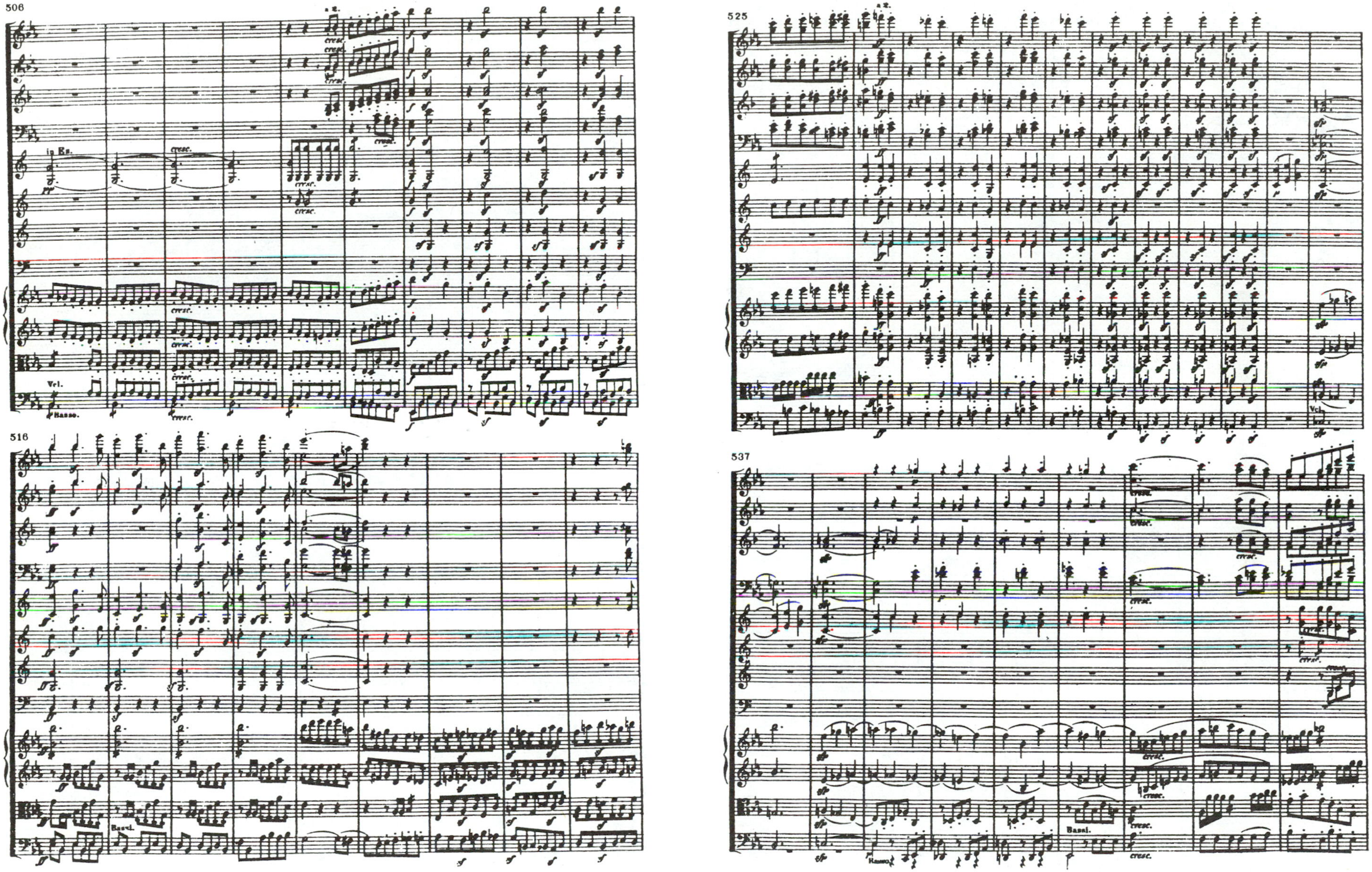
506
a 2.
cresc.
in Es.
Vcl.
Basso.
516
525
537
Bassi.

546
Vel.
Basso.
decresc.
559
decresc.
570
Bassi.
580
same var on 1st theme cs 284
cresc.
pizz.
arco.
Vel.

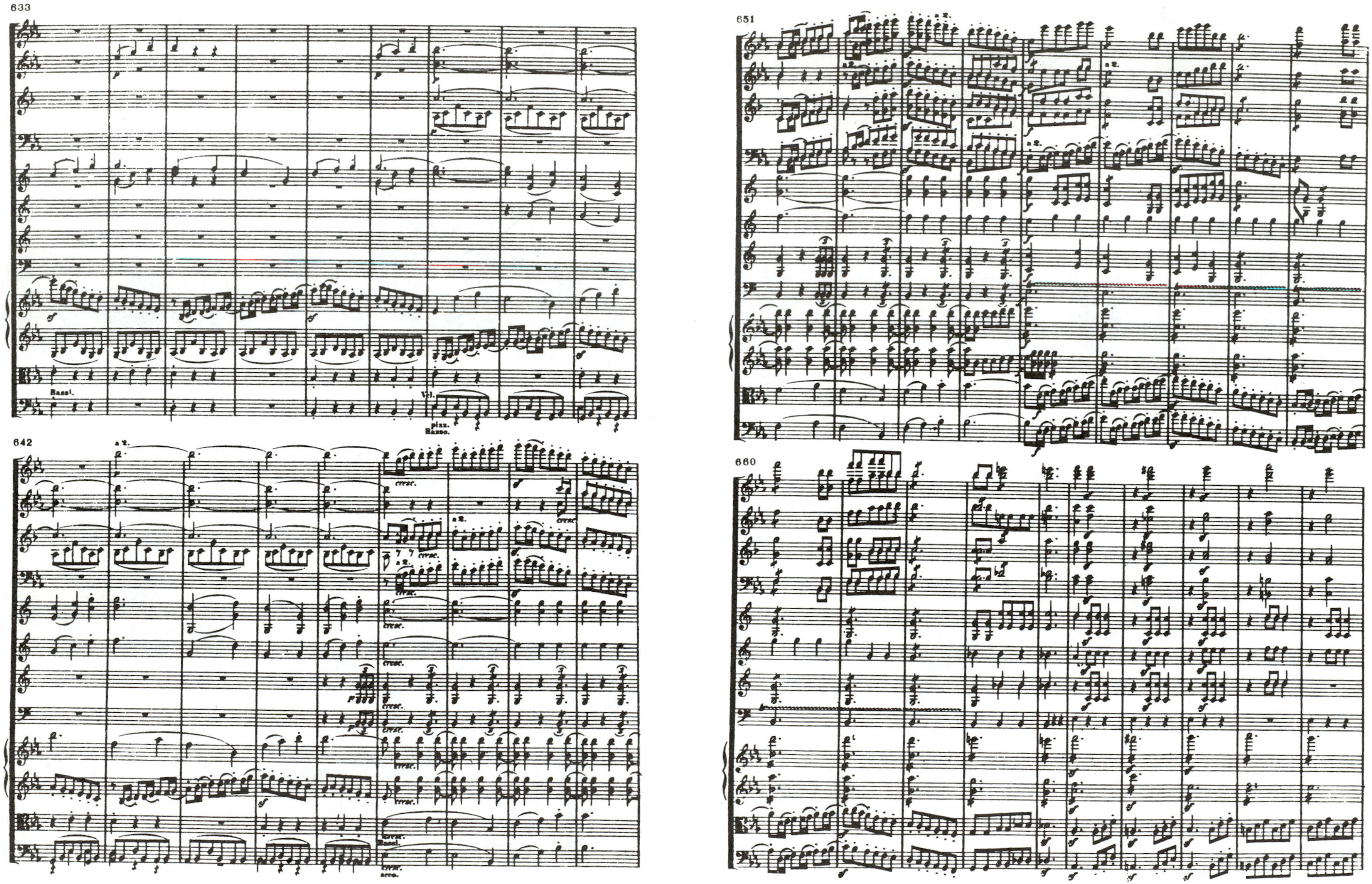
633
Bassi.
pizz.
Basso.
642
a 2.
cresc.
Bassi.
arco.
651
660

139. DER FREISCHÜTZ, Act II, Scene 4 (Finale): The Wolf Glen
Carl Maria von Weber (1786–1826)

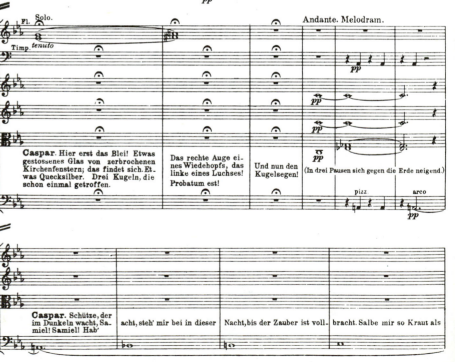

Anmerkung. Die folgenden beiden bis kommen in Anwendung im Fall Max nicht genug Zeit haben sollte.

Clar.
Corni in C.
Timp.
Solo.
Allegro moderato.
Caspar. Blei, segn' es Sieben, Neun und
Drei, dass die Kugel tüchtig
sei!
Samiel! Samiel! her-bei!
pizz.
Vcello.
(Die Masse in der Giess-
kelle fängt an zu gähren und zu zischen, und giebt einen grünlich weissen Schein.
Eine Wolke läuft über den Mondstreif, dass die ganze Gegend nur noch von dem Herdfeuer, den Augen der Eule und dem faulen Holze des Baumes beleuchtet ist.)
Caspar (giesst, lässt die Kugel aus der Form fallen und ruft:
Fl.
(Das Echo
Eins!
wiederholt Eins!)
Fl.
Ob.
Clar.
(Waldvögel kommen herunter, setzen sich um das Feuer, hüpfen und flattern.)
Fl.
Ob.
Clar.
Fag.
Tromb. Basso.
Poco più moto.
a 2.
Caspar (giesst und zählt:) Zwei! (Echo. Zwei!)
Bassi.
(Ein schwarzer Eber raschelt durch's Gebüsch und jagt wild vorüber.)
Clar.
Fag.
Tromb. B.
a 2.
Caspar (scheint zu stutzen und zählt:)...
Clar.
a 2.
Fag. a 2.
Corni in C.
Tromb. B.
Timp.
cresc.
Caspar.
Drei! (Echo. Drei!) (Ein Sturm erhebt sich, beugt und bricht Wipfel der Bäume,

Ob.
Clar. *cresc.*
Fag.
Corni in Es.
cresc.
Corni in C.

jagt Funken vom Feuer u.s.w.)

Fl.

Viol.

Caspar (zählt ängstlich:) Vier! (Echo. Vier!) (Man hört Rasseln, Pritschengeknall und Pferdegetrappel.)

(Vier feurige, funkenwerfende Räder rollen über die Bühne.)

Caspar (immer ängstlicher, zählt:) .... Fünf! (Echo. Fünf!)

Fag.

sempre tutto fortissimo possibile

Corno in B.

Corno in F. *sempre tutto fortissimo possibile*

Corni in E. *sempre tutto fortissimo possibile*

Tromboni.

(Hundegebell und Wiehern in der Luft.)

Chor. (Tenor, Bass unsichtbar.)

(Nebelgestalten von Jägern zu Fuss und zu Ross, Hirsche und Hunde ziehen in der

Durch

Timp.

Höhe vorüber.) Tenor. Bass.

Berg und Thal, durch Schlund und Schacht, durch Thau und Wolken, Sturm und Nacht, durch Thau und Wolken, Sturm und Nacht!

Tromb. B.

Durch Höh_le, Sumpf und Er_den_kluft,__ durch Feu_er, Er_de, See und Luft! Jo_ho, wau wau, jo_ho, wau wau, jo_

Presto.

Fl. pice.

Fl.

Fl.

Ob.

Clar.

a 2.

muta in F.

Trombe in C.

Timp. in C.A.

Tromb. B. ten. Tromboni.

Presto.

ho! ho! ho! ho! ho! ho! ho!

Caspar. Wehe, das wilde Heer!
Sechs! Wehe! (Echo. Sechs! Wehe!) (Der ganze Himmel wird schwarze Nacht.)

Corni in F.

Corni in E.

Trombe.

Timp.

(Die Gewitter treffen furchtbar zusammen. Flammen schlagen aus der Erde. Irrlichter zeigen sich auf den Bergen u.s.w.)

43

Caspar (zuckend und schreiend): Samiel!

Caspar.
Samiel!
(Er wird zu Boden geworfen).

hilf!

Max (gleichfalls vom Sturm hin- und hergeschleudert, springt aus dem Kreis, fasst einen
Ast des verdorrten Baums und schreit):

Samiel!

Sieben!

Samiel (mit furcht-
barer Stimme):

Hier bin ich!
(In demselben Augenblicke fängt das Ungewitter an, sich zu beruhigen, an der Stelle
des verdorrten Baums steht der schwarze
Jäger, nach Maxens Hand fassend).

Max (schlägt ein
Kreuz und stürzt
zu Boden).

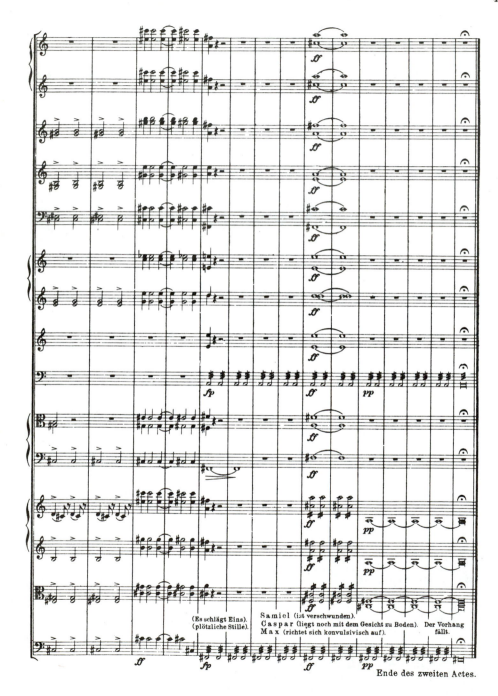

Setting is a dismal wooded glen with gnarled trees and crags. Caspar is making a circle with black boulders.

CHORUS OF SPIRITS:
Upper voices sing: Uhui! Uhui!
   (repeatedly)
Basses:
Milch des Mondes fiel auf's Kraut,
Spinnweb' ist mit Blut betaut!
Eh' noch wieder Abend graut,
Ist sie tot, die zarte Braut!
Eh' noch wieder sinkt die Nacht,
Ist das Opfer dargebracht.
(Die Uhr schlägt ganz in der Ferne 12.
   Der Kreis von Steinen ist vollendet.)
(Caspar reisst heftig den Hirschfänger
   heraus und stösst ihn mitten in den
   Todtenschädel.)
CASPAR (Erhebt den Hirschfänger mit
   dem Todtenkopfe, dreht sich dreimal
   herum u. ruft:)
Samiel! Samiel! erschien'!
Bei des Zaub'rers Hirngebein!
Samiel! Samiel! erschien'!

[NOTE: SAMIEL DOES NOT SING.]

SAMIEL:
Was rufst du mich?
   (Samiel tritt aus einem Felsen.)

CASPAR: (wirst sich nieder)
Du weisst, dass meine Frist schier
   abgelaufen ist.

SAMIEL:
Morgen!

CASPAR:
Verlang're sie noch einmal mir;

SAMIEL:
Nein!

CHORUS OF SPIRITS:
Upper voices: Uhui! Uhui!

Basses:
Milk of the moon fell on plant,
Spiderweb is bedewed with blood!
Before evening darkens again,
she will be dead, the dainty bride!
Before night falls again,
the sacrifice will be offered.
(In the distance a clock strikes 12. The
   circle of stones is complete.)
(Caspar violently yanks out his hunting
   knife and shoves it into the middle of
   a skull.)
CASPAR (raises the hunting knife with
   the skull, turns around three times
   and shouts:)
Samiel! Samiel! appear!
By the sorcerer's skull!
Samiel! Samiel! appear!

SAMIEL:
Why do you call me?
   (Samiel steps out from behind a
   rock.)

CASPAR: (in a lower voice)
You know that my time has almost run
   out.

SAMIEL:
Tomorrow!

CASPAR:
Extend it for me once more;

SAMIEL:
No!

CASPAR:
Ich bringe neue Opfer dir,

SAMIEL:
Welche?

CASPAR:
Mein Jagdgesell, er naht,
Er, der noch nie dein dunkles Reich
    betrat.

SAMIEL:
Was sein Begehr?

CASPAR:
Freikugeln sind's, auf die er Hoffnung
baut.

SAMIEL:
Sechse treffen! Sieben äffen!

CASPAR:
Die siebente sei dein; aus seinem Rohr
    lenk' sie nach seiner Braut!
Dies wird ihn der Verzweiflung weih'n,
    ihn . . . und den Vater.

SAMIEL:
Noch hab' ich keinen Theil an ihr!

CASPAR:
Genügt er dir allein?

SAMIEL:
Das findet sich!

CASPAR:
Doch schenkst du Frist, und wieder auf
    drei Jahr', bring ich ihn dir zur Beute
    dar?!

SAMIEL:
Es sei! bei den Pforten der Hölle!
    Morgen er oder du!
    (Verschwindet indet unter dumpfen
    Donner.)

CASPAR:
I bring you a new victim,

SAMIEL:
Who?

CASPAR:
My hunting companion, he approaches,
he, who has never yet set foot in your
    dark realm.

SAMIEL:
What [is] his desire?

CASPAR:
It is free-shooting bullets, on which he
builds [his] hope.

SAMIEL:
Six hit [the mark]! Seven mocks!

CASPAR:
The seventh be yours; from his gun
    direct it toward his bride!
This will doom him to despair, him . . .
    and [her] father.

SAMIEL:
As yet I have no share in her!

CASPAR:
Is he alone sufficient for you?

SAMIEL:
That may be! [or, We'll find out!]

CASPAR:
However, you grant [me] time, and for
    another three years, [and] I will
    bring him to you as booty?!

SAMIEL:
So be it! by the gates of Hell! Tomorrow
    him or you!
    (He disappears under hollow
    thunder.)

(CASPAR: richtet sich langsam und
    erschopft auf und trocknet sich von
    der Stirn. Der Hirschfänger mit dem
    Todtenkopf ist verschwunden; an
    dessen Stelle ist ein kleiner Heerd
    mit glimmenden Kohlen aus der Erde
    gekommen.)

CASPAR: (sie erblickend)
Trefflich bedient!
    (thut einen Zug aus der Jagdflasche.)

Gesegn'es, Samiel!
    (trinkt)
Er hat mir warm gemacht!
Aber wo bleibt Max? Sollte er
    wortbrüchig werden? Samiel, hilf!

(Caspar geht, nicht ohne Beängstigund,
    im Kreise hin und her. Die Kohlen
    drohen zu verlöschen, er Kniet zu
    ihnen nieder, legt Reiss auf und bläst
    an. Die Eule und andere Vögel heben
    dabei die Flügel, als wollten sie
    anfachen.)

(Das Feuer raucht und knistert.)
(Max wird auf einer Felsenspitze, dem
    Wasserfall gegenuber sichtbar und
    beugt sich in die Schlucht herab.)

MAX:
Ha! Furchtbar gähnt der düst're
    Abgrund!
Welch' ein Grau'n, das Auge wähnt in
    einen Höllenpfuhl zu schau'n!
Wie dort sich Wetterwolken ballen;

der Mond verliert von seinem Schein;
gespenst'ge Nebelbilder wallen,

belebt ist das Gestein,
und hier . . . husch, husch!
fliegt Nachtgevögel auf im Busch!
Rothgraue, narb'ge Zweige strecken
nach mir die Riesenfaust!

(CASPAR rises slowly, totally
    exhausted, and wipes his forehead.
    The hunting knife with the skull has
    disappeared; in its place a small
    group with smouldering coals has
    come out of the earth.)

CASPAR: (noticing)
Excellent service!
    (He takes a drink from his hunting
    flask.)
Bless it, Samiel!
    (He drinks.)
He has made me [feel] warm!
But where is Max? Would he break his
    word? Samiel, help!

(Caspar goes, not without worry, around
    and around the circle. The coals
    threaten to go out, he kneels down by
    them, puts brush on them and blows
    on it. The owl and other birds take
    flight, as it flames.)

(The fire smokes and crackles.)
(Max appears on the edge of a crag
    above the waterfall and looks into the
    glen.)

MAX:
Ha! The gloomy abyss yawns fearfully!

What a horror! the eye imagines it is
    looking into a hellish pool!
How storm clouds are gathering over
    there;
the moon is losing its radiance;
ghostly mist-pictures are floating [in
    air],
the rock has come to life,
and here . . . whish! swish!
night birds fly in and out of the bushes!
Red-grey gnarled branches stretch
    their giant fists toward me!

Nein, ob das Herz auch graust—
ich muss! ich trotze allen Schrecken!
  (Er klettert einige Schritte herab.)

CASPAR: (erblickt ihn)
Dank Samiel! die Frist ist gewonnen!

CASPAR: (zu Max)
Kommst du endlich, Kamerad?
Ist das auch recht, mich so allein zu
  lassen?
Siehst du nicht, wie mir's sauer wird?
  (Er hat das Feuer mit dem
  Adlerflügel angefacht und erhebt
  diesen im Gespräch gegen Max.)

MAX: (nach dem Adlerflügel starrend.)
Ich schoss den Adler aus hoher Luft;
ich kann nicht rückwärts, mein
  Schicksal ruft!
  (Er klettert einige Schritte, bleibt dann
  wieder stehen und blickt starr nach
  dem gegenüberstehenden Felsen.)

MAX:
Weh mir!

CASPAR:
So komm doch! Die Zeit eilt!

MAX:
Ich kann nicht hinab!

CASPAR:
Haasenherz! klimmst ja sonst wie eine
  Gemse!

MAX:
Sieh dort hin, sieh!
  (Er deutet nach dem Felsen; man
  erblickt eine weisse verschleierte
  Gestalt, die die Hände erhebt.)
Was dort sich weist, ist meiner Mutter
  Geist.
So lag sie im Sarg; so ruht sie im Grab.

No, although my heart shudders—
I must! I defy all terror!
  (He descends a few steps.)

CASPAR: (notices him)
Thanks, Samiel! The time is won! [or,
  More time was granted!]

CASPAR: (to Max)
Have you come at last, comrad?
Is it right to leave me so alone?

Do you not see how difficult it is for me?
  (He fanned the fire with an eagle's
  wing, and he raises it while speaking
  to Max.)

MAX: (staring at the eagle's wing)
I shot the eagle out of high air [at great
  height]; I cannot turn back, my
  destiny calls!
  (He descends a few steps, remains
  standing there, and stares fixedly at
  the rocks opposite him.)

MAX:
Woe is me!

CASPAR:
So come then! Time flies!

MAX:
I cannot go down!

CASPAR:
Coward! Once, you climbed like a
  chamois!

MAX:
Look over there, look!
  (He points to the rocks; one notices a
  white veiled figure with its hands
  upraised.)
What is seen there is my mother's ghost.

Thus she lay in her coffin; thus she rests
  in the grave.

Sie fleht mit warnendem Blick, sie winkt
  mir zurück!

CASPAR: (für sich)
Hilf Samiel!
(laut) Alberne Fratzen! Ha! Ha! Ha!
Sieh noch einmal hin, damit du die
  Folgen deiner feiger Thorheit
  erkennst'.

(Die verschleierte Gestalt ist
  verschwunden, man erblickt
  Agathens Gestalt mit aufgelösten
  Locken und wunderlich mit Laub
  und Stroh aufgeputzt. Sie gleicht
  einer Wahnsinnigen, und scheint in
  dem Begriff, sich in den Wasserfall
  hinab zu stürzen.)

MAX:
Agathe! Sie springt in den Fluss! Hinab!
  hinab! ich muss! Agathe! Sie springt
  in den Fluss! Agathe! hinab! ich
  muss! hinab! ich muss!
  (Die Gestalt verschwindet. Max klimmt
  vollends herab; der Mond fängt an
  sich zu verfinstern.)

CASPAR: (höhnisch für sich)
Ich denke wohl auch.

MAX: (heftig zu Caspar)
Hier bin ich, was hab ich zu thun?

CASPAR: (wirst ihm die Jagdflasche
  zu, die Max weglegt)
Zuerst trink' ein mal! Die Nachtluft ist
  kühl und feucht. Willst du selbst
  giessen?

MAX:
Nein, das ist wider die Abrede.

CASPAR:
Nicht? So blieb' ausser dem Kreise,
  sonst kostet's dein Leben!

She implores [me] with a warning
  glance; she waves me back.

CASPAR: (aside)
Help, Samiel!
(aloud) Foolish caricature! Ha! Ha! Ha!
Look again, you will realize the
  consequences of cowardly foolishness.

(The veiled figure has disappeared; one
  sees Agatha's figure with her hair
  mussed and dressed up with leaves
  and straw. She resembles a mad
  woman, and seems about to cast
  herself into the waterfall.)

MAX:
Agatha! She is leaping into the river!
  Down! Down! I must! Agatha! She is
  leaping into the river! Agatha! Down!
  I must! (repeated)
  (The figure disappears. Max descends;
  the moon begins to darken.)

CASPAR: (sneering; aside)
I should think so!

MAX: (vehemently, to Caspar)
Here I am; what must I do?

CASPAR: (throws him the hunting
  flask, which Max lays aside)
First drink a bit! The night air is cool
  and damp. Will you do the casting
  yourself?

MAX:
No, that is against the agreement.

CASPAR:
No? Then stay outside the circle;
  otherwise it costs your life!

MAX:
Was hab' ich zu thun, Hexenmeister?

CASPAR:
Fasse Muth! Was du auch hören und sehen magst, verhalte dich ruhig. (Mit eigenem heimlichen Grausen.) Käme vielleicht ein Unbekannter, uns zu helfen, was kummert's dich? Kommt was anders, was thut's?—So etwas sieht ein Gescheidter gar nicht!

MAX:
O, wie wird das enden!

CASPAR:
Umsonst ist der Tod! Nicht ohne Widerstand schenken verborgene Naturen den Sterblichen ihre Schätze. Nur wenn du mich selbst zittern siehst, dann komme mir zu Hülfe und rufe, was ich rufen werde, sonst sind wir beide verloren.

MAX: (macht ein Bewegung des Einwurfs)

CASPAR:
Still! Die Augenblicke sind kostbar!

(Der Mond ist bis auf einen schmalen Streif verfinstert. Caspar nimmt die Giesskelle.)

Merk' auf, was ich hinein werfen werde, damit du die Kunst lernst! (Er nimmt die Ingredienzen aus der Jagdtasche und wirft sie nach und nach hinein.)

CASPAR:
Hier erst das Blei! Etwas gestossenes Glas von zerbrochenen Kirchenfenstern; das findet sich.

MAX:
What must I do, sorcerer?

CASPAR:
Take courage! Whatever you may see and hear, remain calm. (With his own inner horror.) If, perhaps, a stranger came to help us, what do you care? or, if anything else comes, what does it matter?—A clever man sees nothing like that!

MAX:
Oh, how will it end?!

CASPAR:
Death is free! Not without a struggle do hidden forces of nature yield their treasures to mortals. Only when you see me trembling, then come to help me, and call out what I call out; otherwise we are both lost.

MAX: (makes a gesture of objection)

CASPAR:
Quiet! Moments are precious!

(The moon is reduced to a small strip. Caspar takes the casting ladle.)

Pay attention to what I do, so you learn the art! (He takes the ingredients out of the hunting pouch and throws them in one after another.)

CASPAR:
Here first the lead! Some shattered glass from broken church windows; we'll see. Some quicksilver. Three bullets

Etwas Quecksilber. Drei Kugeln, die schon einmal getroffen. Das rechte Auge eines Wiedehopfs, das linke eines Luchses!
Probatum est!
Und nun den Kugelsegen! (In drei Pausen sich gegen die Erde neigend.)

CASPAR:
Schütze, der im Dunkeln wacht, Samiel! Samiel! Hab' Acht, steh' mir bei in dieser Nacht, bis der Zauber ist vollbracht. Salbe mir so Kraut also Blei, segn' es Sieben, Neun, und Drei, dass die Kugel tüchtig sei! Samiel! Samiel! her bei!

(Die Masse in der Giesskelle fängt an zu gähren und zu zischen, und giebt einen grünlich weissen Schein. Eine Wolke läuft über den Mondstreif, dass die ganze Gegend nur noch von dem Herdfeuer, den Augen der Eule und dem faulen Holze des Baumes beleuchtet ist.)

CASPAR (geisst, lässt die Kugel aus der Form fallen, und ruft):

CASPAR:	ECHO:
Eins!	Eins!
Zwei!	Zwei!

(Ein schwarzer Eber rauschelt durch's Gebüsch und jagt wild vorüber.)

| Drei! | Drei! |

(Ein Sturm erhebt sich beugt und bricht Wipfel der Bäume jagt Funken vom Feuer, u.s.w.)

that already have hit the mark. The right eye of a hoopoe, the left eye of a lynx.

It is proven!
And now the blessing of bullets! (He bows to the earth three times.)

CASPAR:
Marksman, who keeps watch in darkness, Samiel! Samiel! Hear me! Stay by me this night, until the magic spell is completed. Anoint for me both herb and lead, bless it seven, nine, and three times, so that the bullets may be sound! Samiel! Come here!
(The mass in the crucible begins to ferment and hiss, and gives off a greenish light. A cloud passes over the moonstreak, so that the entire glen is illuminated by only the fire, and the owl's eyes and the rotting wood of the trees are seen in the light.)

CASPAR (casts, and as the bullets fall one by one from the mold, cries out):

CASPAR:	ECHO:
One!	One!
Two!	Two!

(A black boar rustles through the bushes and runs past wildly.)

| Three! | Three! |

(A storm gathers, and bends and breaks the top of the tree, and drives sparks from the fire, etc.)

Vier!   Vier!

(Man hört Rasseln, Peitschengeknall
   und Pferdegetrappel.)

Funf!   Funf!

MALE CHORUS:
Durch Berg und Thal, durch Schlund
   und Schacht, durch Thau und
   Wolken, Sturm und Nacht, durch
   Thau und Wolken, Sturm und Nacht!
Durch Höhle, Sumpf und Erdenkluft,
   durch Feuer, Erde, See, und Luft!
Joho! wau wau, joho, wau wau, joho! ho!
   ho! (repeated several times)

CASPAR:
Woho, das wilde Heer!
Sechs! woho!
        ECHO: Sechs! woho!

(Der ganze Himmel wird schwarze
   Nacht.)
(Die Gewitter treffen furchtbar
   zusammen. Flammen schlagen aus
   der Erde. Irrlichter zeigen sich auf
   den Bergen, u.s.w.)

CASPAR: (ruckend und schreiend)

Samiel! Samiel! Hilf!
   (Er wirdzu Boden geworfen.)

Four!   Four!

(One hears rustling, the crack of a whip,
   horses clattering around.)

Five!   Five!

MALE CHORUS:
Through mountain and vale, through
   gorge and ravine, through mist and
   cloud, storm and night, through mist
   and cloud, storm and night!
Through cave, swamp, and chasm,
   through fire, earth, sea, and air!
Yoho! wow, wow, yoho, wow, wow, yoho,
   ho! ho! (etc.)

CASPAR:
Woho! the wild host!
Six! woho!
        ECHO: Six! woho!

(The entire heavens become black
   night.)
(The storm strikes together with terror.
   Flames shoot out of the earth. Will-
   o'-the-wisps show themselves on the
   mountain, etc.)

CASPAR: (moving back and crying
   out):
Samiel! Samiel! Help!
   (He throws himself to the ground.)

MAX:
(gleichfalls von Sturm hin- und
   hergeschleudert, springt aus dem
   Kreis, fasst einen Ast des verdorrten
   Baums und Schreit):
Sieben!   Samiel!

SAMIEL: (mit furchtbarer Stimme):
Hier bin ich!

(In demselben Augenblicke fängt das
   Ungewitter an, sich zu beruhigen, an
   der Stelle des verdorrten Baums steht
   der schwarze Jäger, nach Maxens
   Hand fassend.)

MAX (schlägt ein Kreuz und sturzt zu
   Boden)
   (Es schlagt Eins.)
   (plotzliche Stille)

(Samiel ist verschwanden.)

(Caspar liegt noch mit dem Gesicht
   zu Boden.)

(Max richtet sich konvulsivisch auf.)

Der Vorhang fällt.

End das zweiten Actes.

MAX:
(as the storm hurls itself about, Max
   springs out of the circle, grasps a
   bough of the withered tree, and cries
   out):
Seven!   Samiel!

SAMIEL: (in a frightening voice):
Here am I!

(In the same instant the thunderstorm
   begins to lull, in the place of the
   withered tree stands the black
   hunter, grasping Max's hand.)

MAX (makes sign of the cross and falls
   to the ground)
   (The clock chimes One.)
   (sudden stillness)

(Samiel has disappeared.)

(Caspar still lies with his face to the
   ground.)

(Max stands up, convulsively.)

The curtain falls.

End of the second Act.

140. HEIDENRÖSLEIN, Lied
Franz P. Schubert (1797–1828)

Sah ein Knab' ein Röslein stehn,
Röslein auf der Heiden,
war so jung und morgenschön,
lief er schnell es nah' zu sehn,
sah's mit vielen Freuden.

Röslein, Röslein, Röslein rot,
Röslein auf der Heiden.

Knabe sprach: ich breche dich,
Röslein auf der Heiden.
Röslein sprach: ich steche dich,
dass du ewig denkst an mich,
und ich will's nicht leiden.

Röslein, Röslein, Röslein rot,
Röslein auf der Heiden.

Und der wilde Knabe brach
'sRöslein auf der Heiden.
Röslein wehrte sich und stach,

half ihm doch kein Weh und Ach,
musst' es eben leiden.

Röslein, Röslein, Röslein rot,
Röslein auf der Heiden.
—J. W. von Goethe

*up close, at close range.
**Heiden can be translated as heather, heath, or moor.

A boy saw a little rose standing,
little rose on the heather,
it was so young and morning-beautiful,
[that] he ran fast to see it close,*
viewed it with much pleasure.

Little rose, little rose, little red rose,
little rose on the heather.**

The boy said: "I'll pick you,
little rose on the heather."
The little rose spoke: "I'll prick you,
that you eternally remember me,
and I will not permit it."

Little rose, little rose, little red rose,
little rose on the heather.

And the impetuous boy picked it,
the little rose on the heather.
The little rose defended itself and
    pricked,
however, no wails of woe helped it;
it just had to suffer.

Little rose, little rose, little red rose,
little rose on the heather.

Source: Breitkopf & Härtel, Wiesbaden, Germany.

141. ERLKÖNIG, Lied
Franz P. Schubert (1797–1828)

Source: Breitkopf & Härtel, Wiesbaden, Germany.

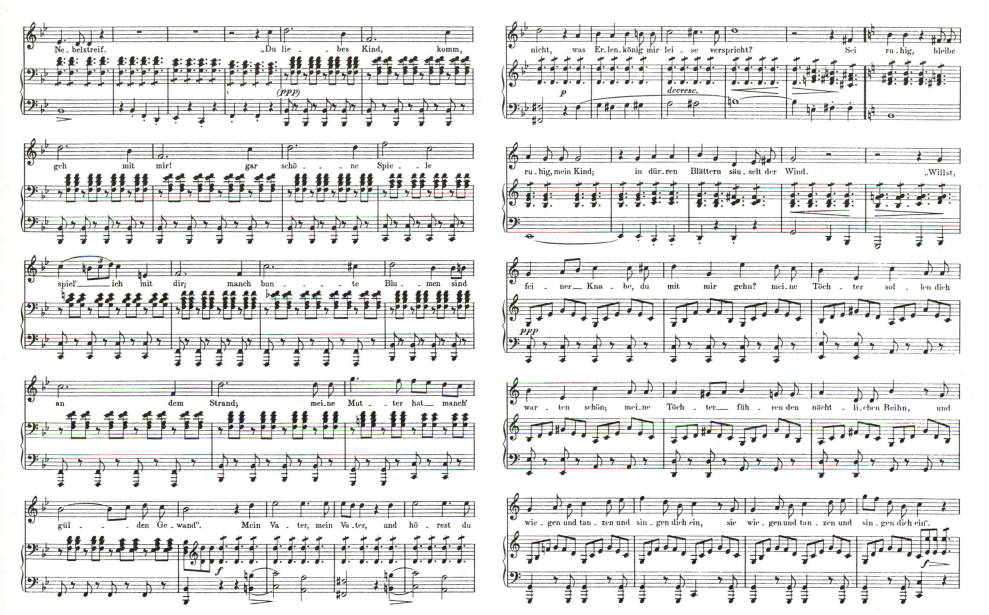

Wer reitet so spät durch Nacht und
 Wind?
Es ist der Vater mit seinem Kind;
er hat den Knaben wohl in dem Arm,
er fasst ihn sicher, er hält ihn warm.

Mein Sohn, was birgst du so bang dein
 besicht?
Siehst, Vater, du den Erlkönig nicht?
Den Erlkönig mit Kron' und Schweif?
Mein Sohn, es ist ein Nebelstreit.

"Du liebes Kind, komm, geh mit mir!
gar schöne Spiele spiel' ich mit dir;
manch' bunte Blumen sind an dem
 Strand;
meine Mutter hat manch' gülden
 Gewand."

Mein Vater, mein Vater, und hörest du
 nicht,
was Erlenkönig mir leise verspricht?
Sei ruhig, bleibe ruhig, mein Kind;
in dürren Blättern säuselt der Wind.

"Willst, feiner Knabe, du mit mir gehn?

mein Töchter sollen dich warten schön;

meine Töchter führen den nächtlichen
 Reihn
und wiegen und tanzen und singen dich
 ein."

Mein Vater, mein Vater, und siehst du
 nicht dort
Erlkönigs Töchter am düstern Ort?

Mein Sohn, mein Sohn, ich seh es
 genau,
es scheinen die alten Weiden so grau.

"Ich liebe dich, mich reizt deine schöne
 Gestalt;
und bist du nicht willig, so brauch' ich
 Gewalt."

Who rides so late through night and
 wind?
It is the father with his child;
he has the boy well in his arms,
he holds him securely, he keeps him
 warm.

"My son, why are you hiding your face
 so fearfully?"
"Father, don't you see the Erlking?
The Erlking with crown and train?"
"My son, it is a streak of mist."

"You dear child, come, go with me!
very nice games I'll play with you;
many multicolored flowers are on the
 shore;
my mother has many golden garments."

"My father, my father, and do you not
 hear
what the Erlking softly promises me?"
"Be quiet, remain quiet, my child;
the wind is rustling in dry leaves."

"My handsome boy, will you come with
 me?
my daughters shall take good care of
 you,
my daughters lead the nightly
 procession*
and shall cradle and dance and sing you
 to sleep."

"My father, my father, and don't you
 see there
The Erlking's daughters in [that] dark
 place?"
"My son, my son, I see it clearly,

the old willows are gleaming so grey."

"I love you, your beautiful figure
 fascinates me;
and if you are not willing, then I will use
 force."

Mein Vater, mein Vater, jetzt fasst er
 mich an!
Erlkönig hat mir ein Leids gethan.

Dem Vater grauset's, er reitet
 geschwind,
er hält in Armen das ächzende Kind,

erreicht den Hof mit Müh' und Noth;

in seinem Armen das Kind war tot.

—J. W. von Goethe

"My father, my father, now he is taking
 hold of me!
The Erlking has hurt me!"

The father shudders, he rides faster,

he holds in [his] arms the groaning
 child,
[he] reaches the courtyard exhausted
 and troubled;
in his arms the child was dead.

*probably, a procession dance

142. IMPROMPTU NO. 3 (D. 935)
Franz P. Schubert (1797-1828)

143. HOFFNUNG, Lied
Luise Reichardt (1779–1826)

Simply and fervently, the 2nd stanza with rapt expression
(Einfach und innig, die 2te Strophe mit dem Ausdruck der Verklärung)

In the time of ro- ses, Hope, thou wear- y heart!
Wenn die Ro- sen blü- hen, hof- fe, lie- bes Herz,

Spring, a balm dis- clo- ses For the keen- est smart.
still und kühl ver- glü- hen wird der hei- sse Schmerz.

Tho' thy grief o'er- come thee, Thru the win- ter's gloom,
Was den Win- ter ü- ber oft un- heil- bar schien,

Thou shalt thrust it from thee, When the ro- ses bloom.
es ent- weicht das Fie- ber, Wenn die Ro- sen blüh'n.

57

Wenn die Rosen blühen,
hoffe, liebes Herz,
still und kühl verglühen
wird der heisse Schmerz.
Was den Winter über
oft enheilbar schien,
es entweicht das Fieber,
wenn die Rosen blüh'n.

Wenn die Rosen blühen,
matt gequältes Herz,
freue dich! wir ziehen
dann wohl himmelwärts.
Ewig dann genesen,
wirst du neu erglüh'n,
wirst ein himmlisch Wesen,
wenn die Rosen blüh'n.

When the roses bloom,
hope, dear heart,
the burning pain will cease,
will become still and cool.
Whatever during the winter
oft seemed incurable,
it escapes [will escape] the fever,
when the roses bloom.

When the roses bloom,
feeble, tormented heart,
rejoice! then, indeed,
we move toward heaven.
Then, forever recovered,
you will have new radiance,
you will become a heavenly being,
when the roses bloom.

144. IL BARBIERE DI SIVIGLIA, Act I, Aria:
"La calunnia è un venticello"
Gioachino Rossini (1792–1868)

This aria is usually sung one tone lower.

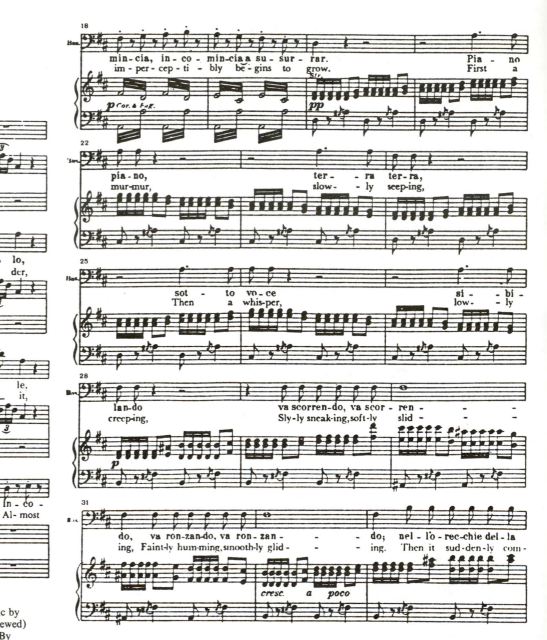

ARIA:

BASILIO:

La calunnia è un venticello,
Un' auretta assai gentille,
Che insensibile, sottile,
Leggermente, dolcemente,
Incomincia, incomincia susurar.

Piano, piano, terra, terra,
Sotto voce, sibilando,
Va scorrendo, va ronzando,
Va scorrendo, va ronzando,
Nelle orecchie della gente
S'introduce, s'introduce destramente,

E le teste, ed i cervelli,
E le teste, ed i cervelli,
Fa stordire, fa stordire, e fa gonfiar.

Della bocca fuori ascendo,
La schiamazzo va crescendo,
Prende forza poco a poco,
Vola già di loco in loco
Sembra il tuono la tempesta,
Che nel sen della foresta
Va fischiando, brontolando,
E ti fa d'orror gelar;
Alla fin trabocca e scoppia,
Si propaga, si raddoppia,
E produce un' esplosione
Come un colpo di cannone,
Come un colpo di cannone,
Un tremoto, un temporale,
Un tremoto generale,
Che fa l'aria rimbombar,
Si, che fa l'aria rimbombar.

E il meschino calcunniato,
Avvilito, calpestato,
Sotto il publico flagello,

Per gran sorte va a crepar.

—Cesare Sterbini

BASILIO:

Slander is a whisper,
A little breeze quite gentle,
That imperceptible, subtle,
Lightly, quietly,
Commences, begins to murmur.

Softly, softly, close to the ground,
In a low voice, hissing,
It flows along, it goes humming,
It goes flying, it goes buzzing,
In the ears of the people
It is introduced, it is slipped in
    dextrously
And the witness, and the brains,
And the testimony, and the sense,
Is made dizzy, is stunned, and is filled
    with air.

Rising from the mouth,
The cackling [or, clamor] increases,
Getting stronger little by little,
It flies, of course, from place to place,
Like the roar of a tempest
That in the bosom of the forest
Goes whistling, rumbling,
And makes you have chills of terror;
Finally, it brims over and it bursts,
So it spreads, so it redoubles,
And creates an explosion
Like a shot from a cannon,
Like a shot from a cannon,
A whirlwind, a thunderstorm,
A general earthquake,
That makes the air reverberate,
Yes, that makes the air re-echo.

And the wretched person slandered,
Humiliated, downtrodden,
Under public beating [= tongue-
    lashing],
Through [this] great destiny is ruined.

145. PRELUDE, Op. 28, No. 4
Frédéric Chopin (1810–1849)

146. ÉTUDE, Op. 25, No. 11, "Winter Wind"
Frédéric Chopin (1810–1849)

Chopin PRELUDE OP. 28, NO. 4, Lea Pocket Scores. Used by kind permission of European American Music Distributors Corporation, agent for Lea Pocket Scores.

Chopin ETUDE OP. 25, NO. 11, Lea Pocket Scores. Used by kind permission of European American Music Distributors Corporation, agent for Lea Pocket Scores.

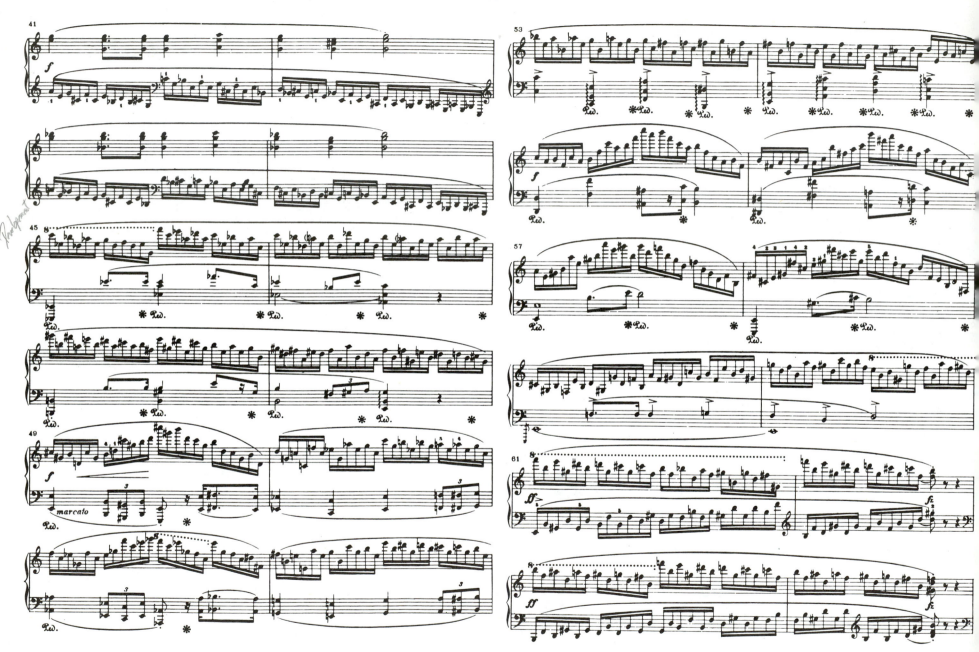

147. NOCTURNE, Op. 32, No. 2
Frédéric Chopin (1810–1849)

148. ELIAS, Oratorio, Nos. 10–16
Felix Mendelssohn (1809–1847)

10. Recitativ mit Chor.

71

11. Chor.

12. Recitativ und Chor.

13. Recitativ und Chor.

15. Quartett.

16. Recitativ und Chor.

149. DER NUSSBAUM, Op. 25, No. 3, Lied
Robert Schumann (1810–1856)

Source: Breitkopf & Härtel, Wiesbaden, Germany.

85

Es grünet ein Nussbaum vor dem Haus,

duftig, luftig, breitet er blättrig die Äste
    aus.
Viel liebliche Blüthen stehen d'ran;
linde Winde kommen; sie herzlich zu
    umfah'n.
Es flüstern je zwei zu zwei gepaart,
neigend, beugend zierlich zum kusse
die Häuptchen zart.
Sie flüstern von einem Mägdlein,
das dächte die Nächte und Tage lang,
wusste, ach! selber nicht, was.
Sie flüstern, wer mag versteh'n so gar
    leise Weis?
flüstern vom Bräut'gam und nächstem
    Jahr.
Das Mägdlein horchet, es rauscht im
    Baum;
sehnend, wähnend, sinkt es
lächelnd in Schlaf und Traum.

—J. Mosen

There is a nut tree greening in front of
    the house,
fragrant, airy, it spreads out the leafy
    boughs.
Many lovely buds stand thereon;
gentle breezes come to embrace them
    affectionately.
Paired, they whisper, two by two,
bending, bowing down gracefully to kiss
the delicate little heads.
They whisper of a young maiden,
who thought the nights and days long,
alas! she knew not what.
They whisper, who can understand such
    very soft music?
[they] whisper of bridegroom and next
    year.
The young maiden listens, it rustles in
    the tree;
longing, hoping, she sinks
smiling into sleep and dream.

150. CARNAVAL, Op. 9, Excerpts
Robert Schumann (1810–1856)

a. Eusebius

Source: Breitkopf & Härtel, Wiesbaden, Germany.

b. **Florestan**

c. **Sphinxes**

No 1. No 2. No 3.

d. **Chiarina**

151. MONDNACHT, Op. 39, No. 5, Lied
Robert Schumann (1810-1856)

Source: Breitkopf & Härtel, Wiesbaden, Germany.

e. Chopin

Es war, als hätt' der Himmel
die Erde still geküsst,
dass sie im Blüthenschimmer

von ihm nur träumen müsst'.

Die Luft ging durch die Felder,
die Ähren wogten sacht,
es rauschten leis' die Wälder,
so sternklar war die Nacht.

Und meine Seele spannte
weit ihre Flügel aus,
flog durch die stillen Lande,
als flöge sie nach Haus.

—Eichendorff

It was as if heaven had
quietly kissed the earth,
that in the flowers' splendor it [i.e.,
    earth]
must dream only of him [i.e., heaven].

The breeze went through the fields,
the [wheat]heads billowed gently,
it softly rustled the woodlands,
so starlit was the night.

And my soul spread
wide its wings,
flew over the silent lands,
as though flying home.

form

A - A₁ - somewhat strophic
(repition - 2 parts) midly

152. LIEBST DU UM SCHÖNHEIT, Lied,
Clara Schumann (1819–1896)

Source: Breitkopf & Härtel, Wiesbaden, Germany.

Liebst du um Schönheit, o nicht mich liebe!	If you love for beauty, oh, do not love me!
Liebe die Sonne, sie trägt ein goldnes Haar!	Love the sun, it wears golden hair!
Liebst du um Jugend, o nicht mich liebe!	If you love for youth, oh, do not love me!
Liebe den Frühling, der jung ist jedes Jahr!	Love the spring, which is young every year!
Liebst du um Schätze, o nicht mich liebe!	If you love for treasures, oh, do not love me!
Liebe die Meerfrau, sie hat viel Perlen klar!	Love the mermaid, she has many bright pearls!
Liebst du um Liebe, o ja, mich liebe!	If you love for love, oh yes, love me!
Liebe mich immer, dich lieb' ich immer, immerdar!	Love me always, [for] I love you always, forevermore!

—Friedrich Rückert

← Fr Protestants - Calvinism - grand opera -

153. LES HUGUENOTS, Act IV, Scenes 22, 23
Giacomo Meyerbeer (1791–1864)

Entr'acte, Recitative, Romanza, and Scene, proceeding directly into Conjuration and Benediction of Daggers

Source: Reprinted from Les Huguenots (Paris: Ph. MAQUET & Cie., not dated.)

92

ROMANZA

CONJURATION

98

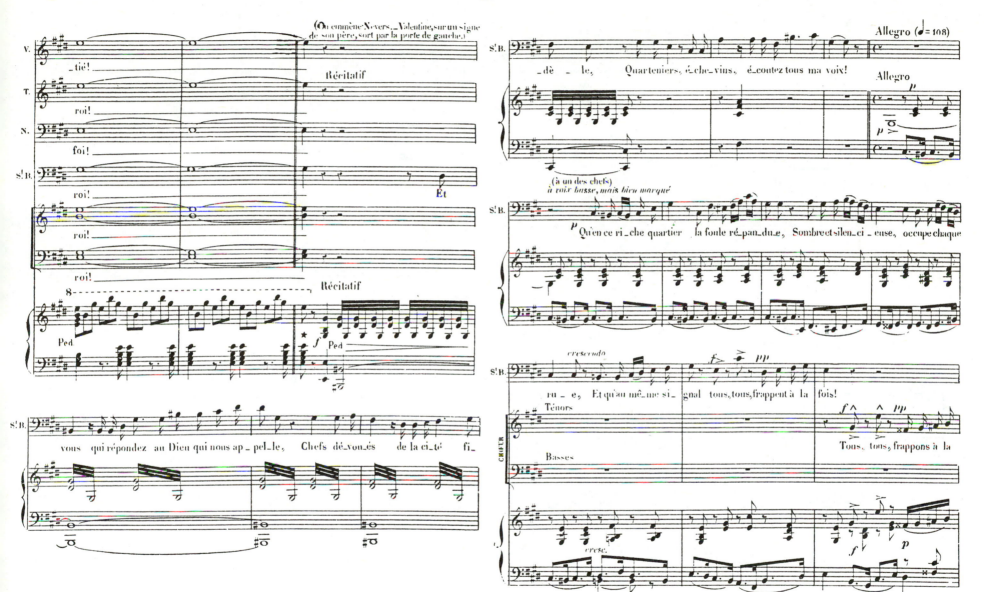

BÉNÉDICTION DES POIGNARDS

Poco andante (♩ = 80)

(Le 1ᵉʳ moine est un Ténor)

TROIS MOINES
Sᵗ BRIS (avec le 3ᵉ moine)

(Les portes du fond s'ouvrent; trois moines, portant des corbeilles, avec des écharpes blanches, s'avancent lentement. Sᵗ Bris revient avec eux.)

PIANO

Poco andante

117

118

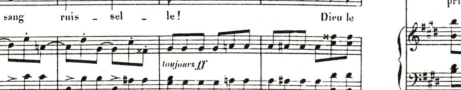

The setting is an apartment in the hotel of Count de Nevers. There are two doors: one leads into Valentine's bedroom; the other, hidden by a tapestry, leads into a study. A window looks out on the street.

VALENTINE
Je suis seul chez moi, seul avec ma
    doulour!
À d'éternels tourments vous m'avez
    condamnée, Mon père!
Un autre avait mon coeur,
Et pourtant vous m'avez donnée!

VALENTINE
I am alone in my home, alone with my
    grief!
You have condemned me to eternal
    torments, my father!
Another had my heart,
And yet you have given me [in
    marriage]!

Et vous que j'implorais en vain dans
    mon malheur,
Vous qui l'avez permis, ce funeste
    hyménée,
Mon Dieu, daignez du moins, pour
    alleger mes maux,
Chasser un souvenir fatal à mon repos!

And You whom I implored in vain in my
    distress,
You who have allowed it, this fatal
    marriage,
My God, deign at least, to alleviate my
    sufferings,
to drive away a memory fatal to my
    peace!

(Valentine sings this ROMANZA)

Parmi les pleurs mon rêve se ranime;
C'est à lui seul qu'appartiennent mes
    jours—mes jours.
Ces doux regrets, y penser est un crime;

je veux les fuir, je veux les fuir,—hélas!
    et j'y pense toujours—toujours!

De loin encor sa voix chérie, oui,
    même ici sa voix chérie
Fait taire en moi la voix des cieux;
Et son image, quand je prie,
Sur les autels, hélas! s'offre, s'offre
    à mes yeux—(repeated)
    s'offre à mes yeux!
Raoul, cher Raoul!
quelle est donc sa puissance?
De Dieu lui-même il est vainqueur!
Ah! que me sert d'éviter sa présence?

Je le retrouve toujours dans mon coeur!
Ah! que me sert . . . (repeated)

Hélas! hélas!
Mon Dieu! je le retrouve toujours, hélas!

Amid the tears, my dream revives;
It is to him alone that my days belong—
    my days.
These sweet regrets, to think of them is
    a crime;
I want to flee from them, (repeated)
    alas! and I think of them always—
    always!
From far away his dear voice, yes,
    even here his dear voice
silences in me the voice of the heavens;
And his image, when I pray,
on the altars, alas! offers itself,
    offers itself to my eyes—(repeated)
    offers itself to my eyes!
Raoul, dear Raoul!
what, then, is his power?
He is the conqueror of God himself!
Ah! what good does it do me to avoid his
    presence?
I find him again always in my heart!
Ah! what good does it do me . . .
    (repeated)
Alas! alas!
My God! I find him again always, alas!

(Raoul appears in the doorway.)

VALENTINE continues:
Juste ciel! est-ce lui?
    lui dont l'aspect terrible
Ainsi que le remords sans cesse me
    poursuit?

VALENTINE continues:
Just heaven! Is it he?
    he, whose terrible appearance,
as well as remorse, pursues me
    incessantly?

RAOUL
Oui, c'est moi! moi, qui
  viens dans l'ombre et dans la nuit,
Ainsi qu'un criminel, dont la peine est
  horrible,
Et qui, las de souffrir, succombe au
  despoir!

VALENTINE
Que voulez-vous de moi?

RAOUL
Rien! j'ai voulu vous voir avant que de
  mourir!

VALENTINE
Qu'entends-je? est-il possible?
Est mon père! et mon mari!

RAOUL
Oui, je pouvais les rencontrer ici;
Je le savais!

VALENTINE
Leur coeur est inflexible;
Ils vous tueraient! Fuyez!

RAOUL
Non, j'attendrai leurs coups!

VALENTINE
Entendez-vous ces pas? Fuyez!

RAOUL
Non, non, je reste . . .
Et si quelque danger . . .

VALENTINE
Mon père! mon époux!
Pour moi . . . pour mon honneur,
  évitez leur courroux!

(She hides Raoul behind the tapestry, in the room at the side.)

RAOUL
Yes, it is I, who
  come in the shadow and in the night,
Just as a criminal, whose suffering is
  horrible,
And who, weary of suffering, succumbs
  to despair!

VALENTINE
What do you want from me?

RAOUL
Nothing! I wanted to see you before I
  die!

VALENTINE
What do I hear? Is it possible?
It is my father! and my husband!

RAOUL
Yes, I might encounter them here;
I knew it!

VALENTINE
Their hearts are inflexible;
They would kill you! Flee!

RAOUL
No, I will await their blows!

VALENTINE
Do you hear those footsteps? Flee!

RAOUL
No, no, I am staying . . .
And if some danger . . .

VALENTINE
My father! my husband!
For me . . . for my honor,
  avoid their wrath!

SCENE: St. Bris, Nevers, Tavannes, and some other Catholic nobles enter.

ST. BRIS
Oui, l'ordre de la reine en ces lieux vous
  rassemble.
L'heure est enfin venue où je dois à vos
  yeux
Devoiler des projets protégés par les
  cieux,
Et dès longtemps conçus par Medicis.

VALENTINE
Je tremble!

ST. BRIS (to Valentine)
Vous, ma fille, sortez!

VALENTINE
Mon père!

NEVERS
Pourquoi donc?
Son zèle ardent pour la foi catholique
Permet que sans danger devant elle on
  explique
De la reine et du ciel les ordres absolus.

ST. BRIS
Yes, the queen's order musters you in
  this locality.
Finally, the hour has come when I must
  reveal to your eyes
some projects protected by heaven,

and conceived a long time ago by
  Medicis.

VALENTINE
I tremble!

ST. BRIS
You, my daughter, leave!

VALENTINE
My father!

NEVERS
But why?
Her ardent zeal for the Catholic faith
allows us, without danger, to explain
  before her
the absolute orders of the queen and of
  heaven.

CONJURATION

SAINT-BRIS (to the Nobles)
Des troubles renaissants et d'une guerre
  impie
Voulez-vous, comme moi, délivrez le
  pays?

4 NOBLES
C'est notre voeu, c'est notre voeu!

SAINT-BRIS
Du trône et du ciel, du ciel, de la patrie,
Voulez-vous, comme moi, frapper les
  ennemis?

SAINT-BRIS
Do you wish, as I do, to deliver the
  country from recurring troubles and
  an impious war?

4 NOBLES
It is our wish!

SAINT-BRIS
Are you willing, as I am, to strike the
  enemies of the throne, of heaven, and
  of the country?

NOBLES
Nous sommes prêts, nous sommes prêts!

SAINT-BRIS
Eh, bien! Du Dieu qui nous protège
Le glaive menaçant est sur eux sus
    pendu;
Des huguenots la race sacrilège
Aura dès aujourd'hui pour jamais
    disparu!

NEVERS
Mais . . . qui les condamne?

SAINT-BRIS
Dieu!

4 NOBLES
Dieu!

NEVERS
Et qui les frappera?

SAINT-BRIS
Nous!

NOBLES
Nous!

NEVERS
Nous? Nous?

SAINT-BRIS
Pour cette cause sainte
J'obéirai sans crainte,
J'obéirai sans crainte
À mon Dieu, à mon Dieu, à mon roi.
Comptez sur mon courage;
Entre vos mains j'engage,
Entre vos mains j'engage
Mes serments, mes serments et ma foi,
    mes serments et ma foi.

NOBLES
We are ready!

SAINT-BRIS
Well! For God, who protects us,
the menacing sword is suspended over
    them;
The sacrilegious race of Huguenots
from this day will have disappeared
    forever!

NEVERS
But . . . who condemns them?

SAINT-BRIS
God!

NOBLES
God!

NEVERS
And who will strike them?

SAINT-BRIS
We!

NOBLES
We!

NEVERS
We? We will?

SAINT-BRIS
For this holy cause
I will obey without fear,
I will obey without fear
for my God, for my God, for my king.
Count on my courage;
Into your hands I place,
Into your hands I place
my oaths, my vows and my faith, my
    vows and my faith.

ENSEMBLE: Nevers, St.-B., Tavannes, Nobles, and Valentine

Together

NEVERS
Quel est donc ce langage?
À l'honneur seul j'engage
mes serments et ma foi!

TAVANNES, SAINT-BRIS
Comptez sur mon courage!
Entre vos mains j'engage
Mes serments, et ma foi,
À mon Dieu, à mon roi.

NOBLES
Grand Dieu, sauvez, sauvez la foi!
Dieu, sauvez, Dieu, sauvez notre foi,
    sauvez la foi!
J'obéis à mon roi! à mon roi!

VALENTINE
Comment tromper leur rage?
Dieu, soutiens mon courage,
Et prends pitié de moi, pitié, pitié de
    moi!
Ah, grand Dieu, prends pitié! (repeat
    the line)

SAINT-BRIS
Le roi peut-il compter sur vous?

NOBLES
Nous le jourons!

SAINT-BRIS
C'est moi qui dois guider vos pas!

NOBLES
Nous vous suivrons!

ALL BUT NEVERS
Quoi! Nevers seul a gardé le silence!

Together

NEVERS
What language is this?
To honor alone I pledge
my vows and my faith!

TAVANNES, SAINT-BRIS
Count on my courage!
Into your hands I place
my vows, and my faith,
For my God, for my king.

NOBLES
Almighty God, save, save the faith!
God, save, God, save our faith, save our
    faith!
I obey my king! for my king!

VALENTINE
How can I cheat their rage?
God, uphold my courage,
and have pity on me, pity, pity on me!

Ah, almighty God, have pity! (repeat
    the line)

SAINT-BRIS
Can the king count on you?

NOBLES
We swear it!

SAINT-BRIS
It is I who must guide your steps!

NOBLES
We will follow you!

ALL BUT NEVERS
What! Only Nevers kept silent!

VALENTINE
Que va-t-il dire? Je tremble, hélas!

NEVERS
Frappons nos ennemis, mais non pas
    sans défense.
Ce n'est pas le poignard qui doit percer
    leur sein!

SAINT-BRIS
Quand le roi le commande!

NEVERS
Il me commande en vain
De flétrir de mon sang l'honneur et la
    bravoure,
Et parmi ces illustres aïeux dont la
    gloire ici m'entoure,
Je compte des soldats, je compte des
    soldats et pas un assassin!

SAINT-BRIS
Quoi! par toi notre cause est trahie et
    trompée!

NEVERS
Non! mais du deshonneur je sauve mon
    épée!

(He breaks his sword.)

Tiens! tiens! la voilà!
Que Dieu juge entre nous!

VALENTINE (going to Nevers)
Ah! d' aujourd'hui tout mon sang est à
    vous, oui, d'aujourd'hui tout mon
    sang est à vous!
Vous saurez tout; venez, venez, venez,
    venez,
je dois vous apprendre . . .

(The main doors open, revealing officials, all armed.)

VALENTINE
What is he going to say? I tremble, alas!

NEVERS
Let us strike our enemies, but not
    without defense.
It is not the dagger that should pierce
    their breast!

SAINT-BRIS
Whenever the king commands it!

NEVERS
He commands me in vain
To stain with my blood honor and
    bravery,
And among the illustrious ancestors
    whose glory surrounds me,
I count some soldiers, I count some
    soldiers and not one assassin!

SAINT-BRIS
What! By you our cause is betrayed and
    cheated!

NEVERS
No! but I save my sword from dishonor!

See! Really! That's it!
Let God judge between us!

VALENTINE
Ah! from today all my blood is yours,
    yes, from today all my blood is yours!

You shall know everything; come,
    (repeated)
I must inform you . . .

SAINT-BRIS, to the people, and
    pointing to Nevers:
Assurez-vous de lui, de Nevers, de mon
    gendre;
Jusqu'à demain vous m'en répondez
    tous!

VALENTINE (aside)
Puisse le ciel désarmer son courroux!
    Ah! . . .

NEVERS
Ma cause est juste et sainte!

SAINT-BRIS, TAVANNES, NOBLES
Pour cette cause sainte . . .

Together

NEVERS
Je puis, je dois sans crainte, . . .

VALENTINE
D'une mortelle crainte . . .

THE OTHERS
J'obéirai sans crainte, . . .

Together

NEVERS
je puis, je dois sans crainte, . . .

VALENTINE
Mon âme est atteinte!

Together

TAVANNES, SAINT-BRIS
. . . sans crainte à mon Dieu, à mon roi!

VALENTINE
Grand Dieu, prends pitié de moi!

NEVERS
. . . résister à moi roi!

THE OTHERS
. . . à notre roi, . . .

SAINT-BRIS
Take care of him, of Nevers, of my son-
    in-law;
Until tomorrow, all of you will answer to
    me!

VALENTINE
May heaven disarm his wrath!
    Ah! . . .

NEVERS
My cause is just and sacred!

SAINT-BRIS, TAVANNES, NOBLES
For this sacred cause . . .

Together

NEVERS
I can, I must without fear. . .

VALENTINE
By a mortal fear . . .

THE OTHERS
I will obey without fear, . . .

Together

NEVERS
I can, I must without fear, . . .

VALENTINE
My soul is stricken!

Together

TAVANNES, SAINT-BRIS
. . . without fear, for my God, for my
    king!

VALENTINE
Great God, have pity on me!

NEVERS
. . . oppose my king!

THE OTHERS
. . . for our king, . . .

NEVERS
Je le puis, je le dois, . . .

SAINT-BRIS
Recevez . . .

VALENTINE
Ah! grand Dieu, . . .

THE OTHERS
. . . à mon Dieu, . . .

Together

SAINT-BRIS
. . . mes serments et ma foi,
et ma foi!

VALENTINE
prends pitié! (repeated)

NEVERS
. . . résister à mon roi!

THE REST
. . . à mon roi! (repeated)

Together

NEVERS
I can [do] it, I must [do] it, . . .

SAINT-BRIS
Receive . . .

VALENTINE
Oh! Almighty God, . . .

THE OTHERS
. . . for my God, . . .

Together

SAINT-BRIS
. . . my vows and my faith,
and my faith!

VALENTINE
have pity!

NEVERS
. . . oppose my king!

THE REST
. . . for my king!

Together

(Some men lead Nevers away; Valentine's father signals her to leave, and she exits.)

SAINT-BRIS
Et vous qui repondez au Dieu qui nous
    appelle,
chefs dévoués de la cité fidèle,
quarteniers, échevins, écoutez tous ma
    voix!
Qu'en ce riche quartier la foule
    répandue,
Sombre et silencieuse, occupe chaque
    rue,
Et qu'au même signal tous, tous,
    frappent à la fois!

CHORUS
Tous, tous, frappons à la fois!

SAINT-BRIS
And you who answer God, who calls
    you,
devoted heads of the faithful city,
mayors, magistrates, all listen to my
    voice!
Let the crowd circulate in this wealthy
    quarter,
somber and silent, occupy each street,

and, at the same signal, all, all, strike at
    the same time!

CHORUS
All, all, strike at the same time!

SAINT-BRIS
Toi, de Besme, et les tiens, entourez la
    demeure
De l'amiral; que le premier il meure!

CHORUS
Qu'il meure le premier!

SAINT-BRIS to another person
Vous, à l'hôtel de Nesle, où de nos
    ennemis
Tous les principaux chefs ce soir sont
    réunis
À la fête qu'on préparé
Pour Marguerite et le roi de Navarre.

CHORUS
Nous, à l'hôtel de Nesle!

SAINT-BRIS
Écoutez! écoutez! Lorsque de Saint
    Germain
Pour la première fois retentira l'airain,
Attentifs et muets à ce signal d'alarmes,
Dans l'ombre préparez vos soldats et vos
    armes.
Mais à ce lugubre appel, toi, cours
    partout éveiller le beffroi.
Je m'en remets à ta prudence!
Et lorsqu' enfin de l'Auxerrois
La cloche sainte aura pour la seconde
    fois
Du ciel impatient annoncé la vengeance,

Le fer en main, alors, levez-vous tous!
Que tout maudit expire sous vos coups!

Ce Dieu qui vous entend et vous béint
    d'avance,
Soldats chrétiens, marchera devant tous!

SAINT-BRIS
You, de Besme, and your people,
    surround the home
of the admiral; let him die first!

CHORUS
Let him die first!

SAINT-BRIS
You, to the hotel de Nesle, where all the

principal leaders of our enemies are
    assembled this evening
at the feast which they prepared
for Marguerite and the King of
    Navarre.

CHORUS
We, to the hotel de Nesle!

SAINT-BRIS
Listen! listen! When the bronze [bell]
    from
Saint Germain rings for the first time,
attentive and silent at this alarm signal,
in the dark prepare your soldiers and
    your arms.
But, at this lugubrious summons, you,
    run everywhere to sound the alarm.
I am relying on your prudence!
And when, finally, from Auxerrois
the sacred bell will have, for the second
    time
announced the vengeance of impatient
    heaven,
then, sword in hand, all rise!
Let all the accursed die under your
    blows!
This God who hears you and blesses you
    in advance,
Christian soldiers, will march before
    you!

VALENTINE (looking out of her apartment)
Mon Dieu! Mon Dieu! comment le secourir?
Il doit entendre, hélas! et ne peut fuir!
Je veux, je veux et n'ose auprès de lui courir . . .
Dieu tout puissant! dans ce péril extrême
Sauvez Raoul, saùvez Raoul, et n'exposez que moi-même!

VALENTINE
My God! My God! how can I help him?

He must hear, alas! and he cannot flee!
I want, I want and I do not dare to run to his side . . .
Omnipotent God! in this extreme peril

save Raoul, save Raoul, and expose only me!

(Valentine withdraws.)

BENEDICTION OF DAGGERS
(3 monks enter from back of stage and advance slowly.)

MONKS and SAINT-BRIS
Gloire, gloire au grand Dieu vengeur!
Gloire au guerrier fidèle,
Dont le glaive étincelle
Pour servir le Seigneur, (repeat last 2 lines)!

MONKS and SAINT-BRIS
Glory, glory to the great avenger God!
Glory to the faithful warrior,
whose sword flashes
to serve the Lord, (repeat last 2 lines)!

(All present who have swords draw them, and the monks bless swords and daggers.)

Glaives pieux! saintes épées,
Qui dans un sang impur serez bientôt trempées,
Vous par qui le Très-Haut frappe ses ennemis,
Glaives pieux, par nous soyez bénis! Oui,
ALL
gloire au Dieu vengeur, (repeated)!

Pious swords! sacred rapiers,
that soon will be steeped in an impure blood,
you through whom the Most High strikes his enemies,
pious swords, be blessed by us! Yes,
ALL
glory to the avenger God, (repeated)!

(The first 4 lines sung by Saint-Bris and Monks are now sung by all.)

SAINT-BRIS
Que cette écharpe blanche et cette croix sans tache
Du ciel, du ciel distinguent les élus!

SAINT-BRIS
Let this white scarf and this unblemished cross
distinguish heaven's elect!

3 MONKS and SAINT-BRIS
Ni grâce, ni pitié!
Frappez tous sans relâche.
L'ennemi qui s'enfuit, l'ennemi qui se cache,

ALL OTHERS
Frappons, (repeat 5 times more)!

ST.-BRIS and MONKS
Le guerrier suppliant à vos pieds abattu!

ALL OTHERS
Frappons, (repeat 2 times more)!

SAINT-BRIS and MONKS
Ni grâce, ni pitié!
Que le fer et la flamme,
Atteignent le vieillard et l'enfant et la femme!
Anathème sur eux!

ALL ON STAGE
Anathème sur eux!

SAINT-BRIS and MONKS
Dieu ne les connaît pas!

ALL
Dieu le veut, Dieu l'ordonne!
Non! non! grâce à personne!
À ce prix il pardonne
Au pêcheur, au pêcheur répentant.
Que le glaive étincelle,
Que le sang ruiselle,
Et la palme immortelle
Dans le ciel vous attend!
    (1st 4 lines are repeated)
Dieu le veut, Dieu l'ordonne,
N'épargnons personne!
    (various lines are repeated)

SAINT-BRIS
Silence, mes amis!

MONKS and SAINT-BRIS
Neither mercy, nor pity!
Strike all without interruption.
The enemy who flees, the enemy who hides,

ALL OTHERS
Strike, (repeated)!

SAINT-BRIS and MONKS
The fallen warrior pleading at your feet!

ALL OTHERS
Strike, (repeated)!

SAINT-BRIS and MONKS
Neither mercy, nor pity!
Let the sword and the fire
reach old man, child, and woman!

A curse on them!

ALL ON STAGE
Anathema on them!

SAINT-BRIS and MONKS
God does not know them!

ALL
God wills it, God ordains it!
No! no! mercy for no one!
At this price he pardons
the sinner, the repentant sinner.
Let the sword flash,
let the blood flow,
and the immortal palm
awaits you in heaven!
    (1st 4 lines are repeated)
God wills it, God ordains it,
Spare no one!
    (various lines are repeated)

SAINT-BRIS
Silence, my friends!

FIRST MONK
Silence, mes amis!

SAINT-BRIS
Que rien ne nous trahisse!

FIRST MONK
Que rien ne nous trahisse!

SAINT-BRIS and FIRST MONK
Retirons-nous sans bruit!

ALL OTHERS
Pour cette cause sainte

SAINT-BRIS, MONK, CHORUS
J'obéirai sans crainte, (line is repeated)

À mon Dieu, à mon Dieu, à mon roi!
Comptez sur mon courage;
Entre vos mains j'engage, (line is
    repeated)
Mes serments, mes serments et ma foi!

(They begin to leave, slowly.)

FIRST MONK
À minuit!

OTHERS
À minuit!

FIRST MONK
Point de bruit!

OTHERS
Point de bruit!

FIRST MONK
Silence, my friends!

SAINT-BRIS
Let nothing betray us!

FIRST MONK
Let nothing betray us!

SAINT-BRIS and FIRST MONK
Withdraw without noise!

ALL OTHERS
For this holy cause

SAINT-BRIS, MONK, CHORUS
I will obey without fear, (line is
    repeated)
for my God, for my God, for my king!
Rely on my courage;
Into your hands I place, (line is
    repeated)
My oaths, my vows and my faith!

FIRST MONK
At midnight!

OTHERS
At midnight!

FIRST MONK
No noise!

OTHERS
No noise!

Together

SOME IN CHORUS SING:
Que rien ne nous trahisse
Et que de leur supplice
Rien ne les avertisse!
Retirons-nous!

OTHERS IN CHORUS SING:
À minuit! Point de bruit!

ALL
Dieu veut! Oui!

BASSES
À minuit!

Together

SOME IN CHORUS SING:
Let nothing betray us
and let nothing warn them
of their agony!
Withdraw!

At midnight! No noise!

ALL
God wills! Yes!

BASSES
At midnight!

(After all of the men have left the stage, Raoul comes out from behind the tapestry; Valentine comes out of her room; they sing the Grand Duo.)

Very cool, Powerful

154. SYMPHONIE FANTASTIQUE, mvt. 5
"Songe d'une Nuit du Sabbat"
Hector Berlioz (1808–1869)

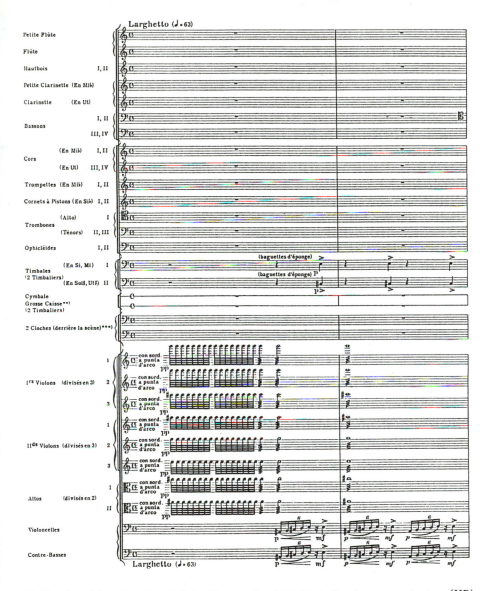

Berlioz - separates many of the voices. Not integrated as Beethoven is

Kind of Rondo form

**) Placed upright and used as timbale. The second and third timbaliers have sponge beaters. (HB)
***) If one cannot find 2 bells deep enough for the C and the G written, it is better to use several pianos on the proscenium. They will perform the bell part in double octaves, as written. (HB)

C
21
Allegro (♩.=112)
P. Fl.
Fl.
Hb.
Cl. (Ut)
Bns
solo lointain
ppp
tr
cresc. poco a poco
Cors (Ut)
III
Tromb.
Oph.
Timb.
(sur les deux timbales)
p
G. C.
senza sord.
Vns
I
II
Altos
Vlles
C.-B.
Allegro (♩.=112)

D
Allegro assai (𝅝 = 76)
29
P. Fl.
Fl.
Hb.
unis.
P. Cl. (Mi♭)
Cl. (Ut)
Bns I-IV
ff
(pavillons en l'air)
(Mi♭)
Cors
(Ut)
(ouvert avec les cylindres)
Tromp. (En Mi♭)
C. à P. (Si♭)
Tromb.
Oph.
Timb.
G. C.
Vns
I
II
Altos
Vlles
C.-B.
Allegro assai (𝅝 = 76)

59
F
P. Fl.
Fl.
Hb.
P. Cl. (Mib)
Cl. (Ut)
Bns
(Mib)
Cors
(Ut)
Vns
Altos
Vlles
unis.
nat.
nat.
mf
cresc.
cresc.
cresc.
cresc.
64
P. Fl.
Fl.
Hb.
P. Cl. (Mib)
Cl. (Ut)
Bns
(Mib)
Cors
(Ut)
Vns
Altos
Vlles
C.-B.
ff

69
G
P. Fl.
Fl.
Hb.
P. Cl. (Mib)
Cl. (Ut)
Bns
unis.
(Mib)
Cors
(Ut)
Tromp. (Mib)
C. à P. (Sib)
Tromb.
Oph.
Timb.
Vns
Altos
Vlles
C.-B.
ff
(baguettes de bois recouvert en peau)
(baguettes de bois recouvert en peau)

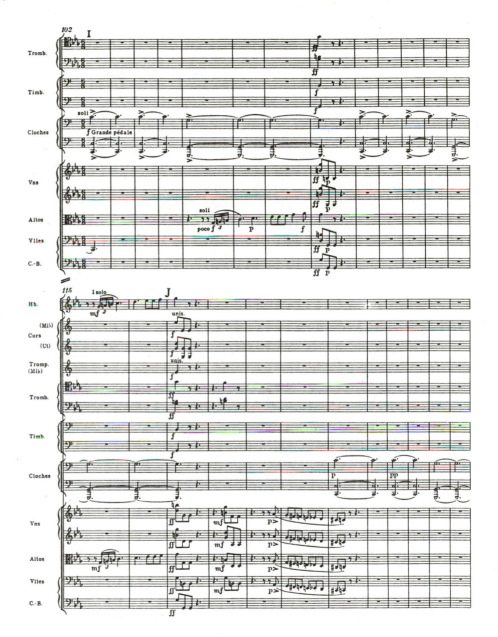

136

Dies Irae
(Day of wrath)

Bells = chant melody
like Mozart's Requiem Mass

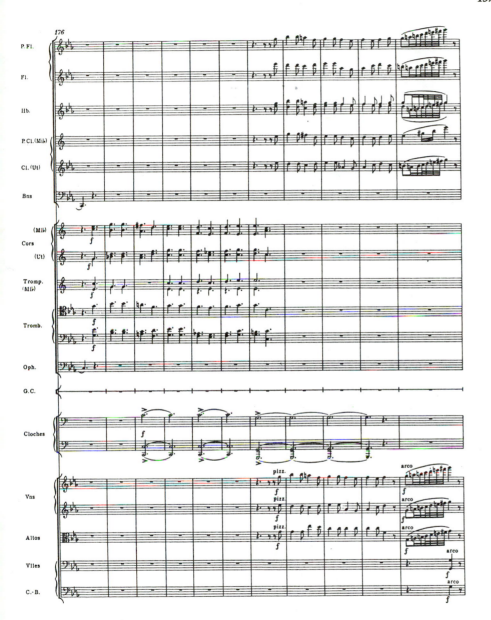

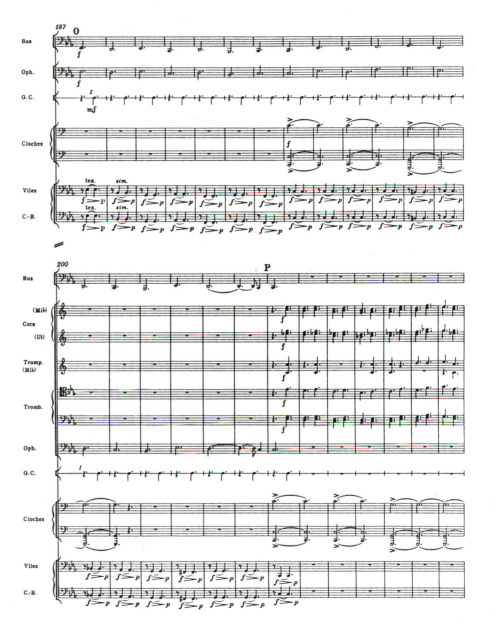

Ronde du Sabbat

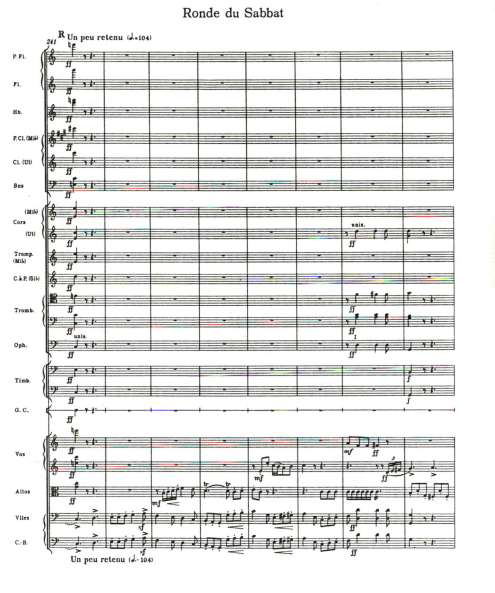

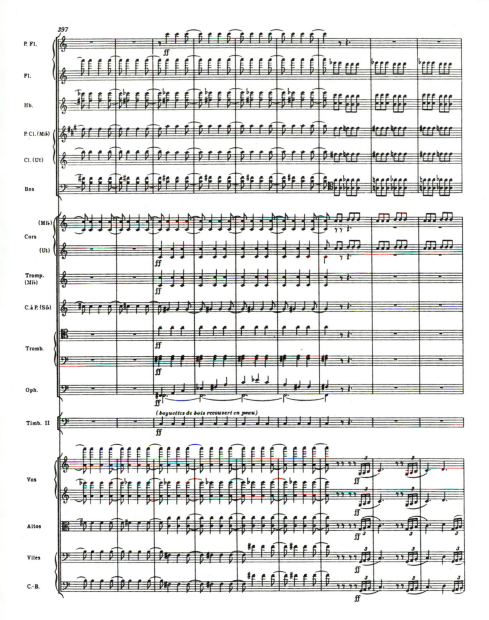

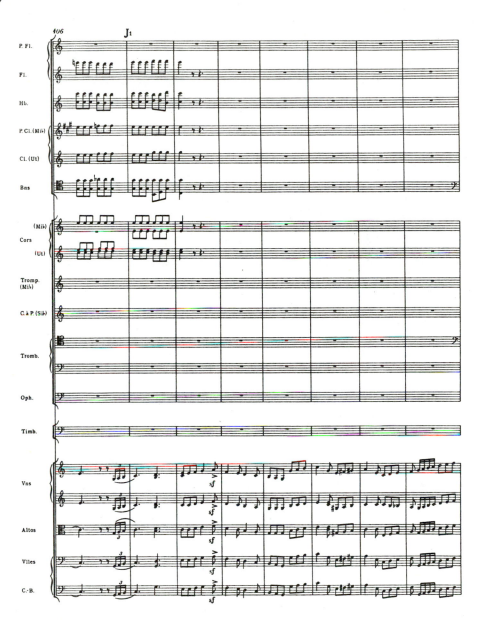

Dies Irae et Ronde du Sabbat ensemble

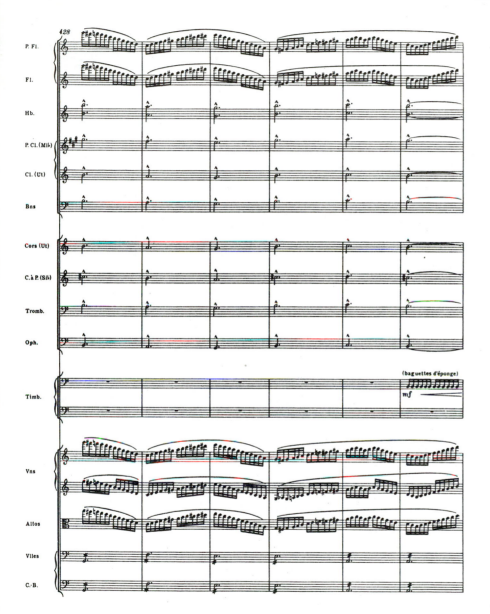

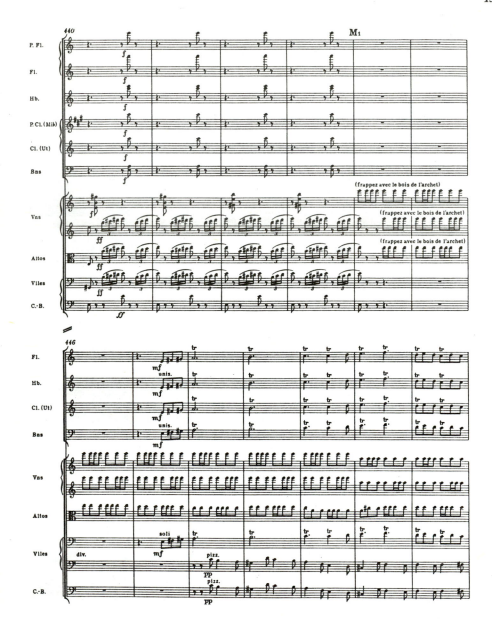

483
Q1
P. Fl.
Fl.
Hb.
P. Cl. (Mib)
Cl. (Ut)
Bns
unis.
(Mib)
Cors
(Ut)
Tromp. (Mib)
C. à P. (Sib)
Tromb.
Oph.
cresc. molto
Timb.
G. C.
(deux timbaliers)
Vns
Altos
Vlles
C.-B.
492
R1
animez
II

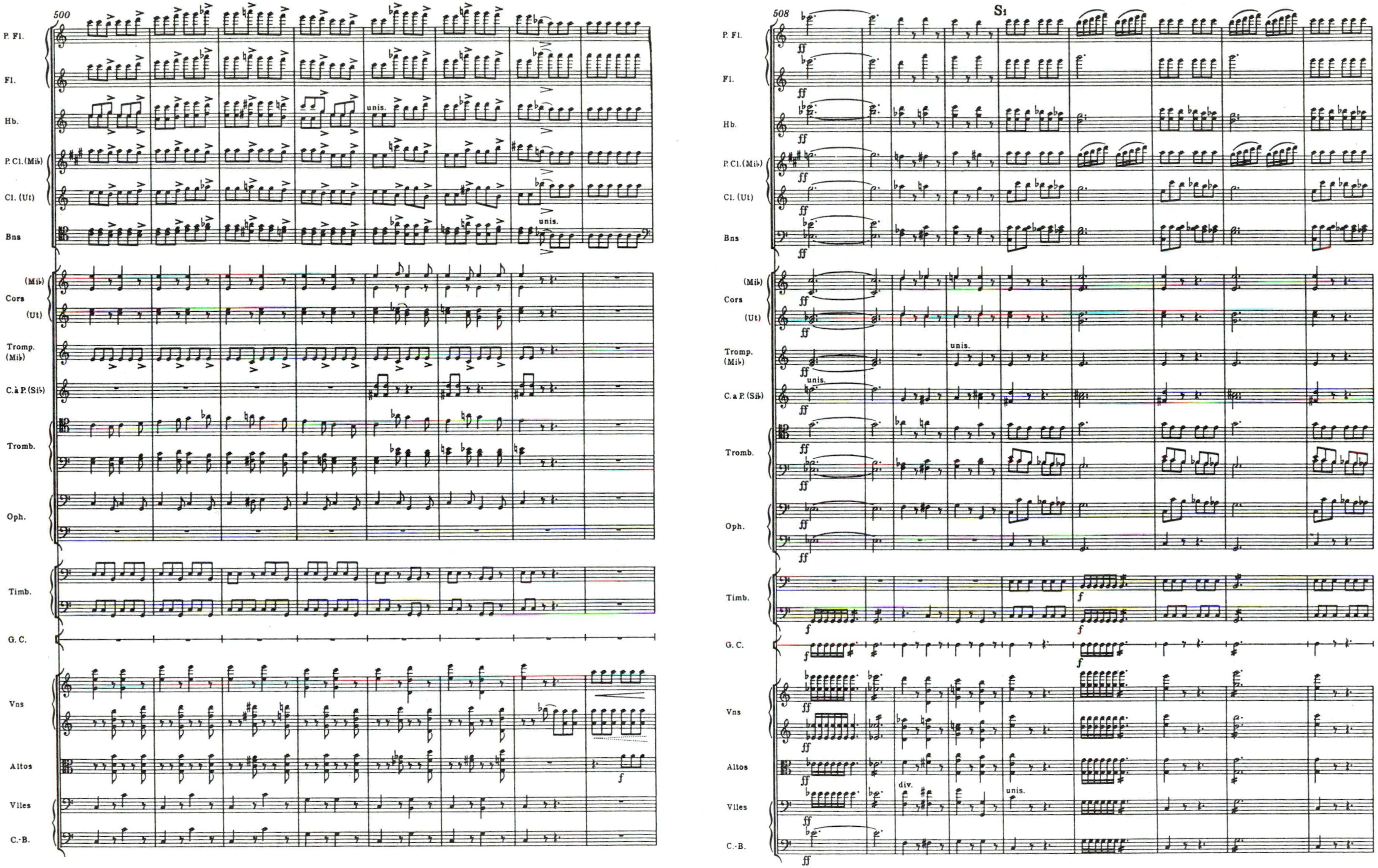
500
P. Fl.
Fl.
Hb.
P. Cl. (Mib)
Cl. (Ut)
Bns
unis.
(Mib)
Cors
(Ut)
Tromp. (Mib)
C. à P. (Sib)
Tromb.
Oph.
Timb.
G. C.
Vns
Altos
Vlles
C.-B.
f
508
S1
ff
unis.
div.
f

155. NORMA, Act II, Scene 4, Scena e Cavatina: "Casta diva"
Vincenzo Bellini (1801-1835)

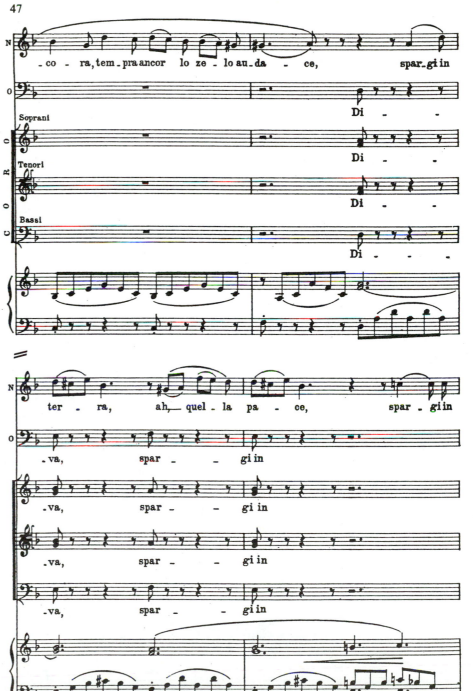

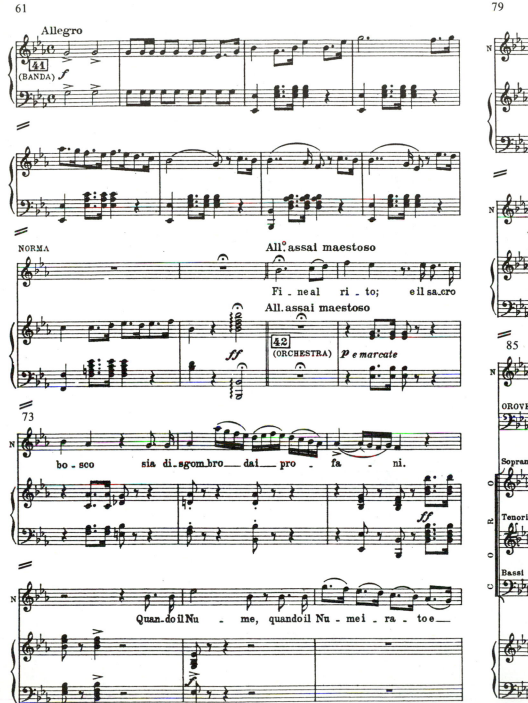

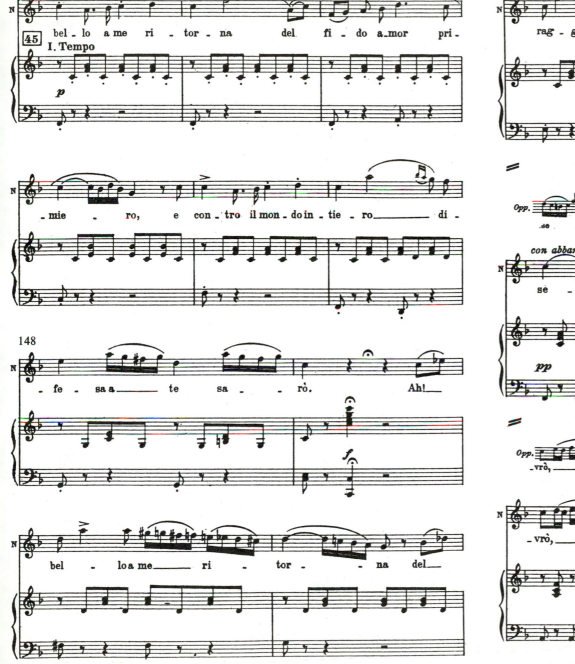

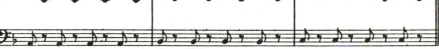

NORMA:

Casta diva, che inargenti
queste sacre antiche piante,
a noi volgi il bel sembiante,
senza nube e senza vel.

NORMA:

Chaste goddess, who silvers
these sacred ancient plants,
turn your lovely gaze on us,
unclouded and unveiled.

(Stanza is repeated by Oroveso and Chorus)

NORMA (joined by Oroveso and Chorus):

Tempra, o Diva, tu de' cori ardenti,

tempra ancora lo zelo audace,
spargi in terra, ah, quella pace
che regnar tu fai nel ciel.

Temper, o goddess, you of the ardent
   hearts,
temper more the bold zeal,
diffuse on earth, ah, that peace
that you make reign in heaven.

NORMA:

Fine al rito; e il sacro bosco

sia disgombro dia profani.
Quando il Nume irato e fosco
chiegga il sangue dei Romani,
dal druidico delubro
la mia voce tuonerà.

NORMA:

The rite is finished; and let the sacred
   woods
be cleared of laymen. [or, profane ones]
When the angry and gloomy god
demands the blood of the Romans,
from the druid shrine
my voice will thunder forth.

OROVESO and Chorus:

Tuoni, e un sol del popol empio

non isfugga al giusto scempio;
e premier da noi percosso
il Proconsole cadrà.

OROVESO and Chorus:

Let it thunder forth, and let not one of
   the
impious people escape the just slaughter;
and at the first of our blows
the Proconsul will fall.

NORMA:

Cadrà . . . punirlo io posso . . .
(Ma punirlo il cor non sa.)

NORMA:

He will fall . . . I can punish him . . .
(But [my] heart doesn't know how to
   punish him.)

(Ah! bello a me ritorna
del fido amor primiero:
e contro il mondo intiero
difensa a te sarò.
Ah! bello a me ritorna
del raggio tuo sereno;
e vita nel tuo seno
e patria e cielo avrò.)

(Ah! love, return to me
the faithful first love:
and against the entire world
your defense I will be.
Ah! love, return to me
your serene ray [= gaze];
and life in your bosom
and [both] a native land and heaven I
   will have.)

OROVESO and Chorus:

Sei lento, sì, sei lento,
o giorno di vendetta;
ma irato il Dio t'affretta
che il Tebro condannò.

OROVESO and Chorus:

You are slow, yes, you are slow,
oh day of revenge;
but the angry god hurries you
whom the Tiber condemned.

NORMA sings again the text "Ah! bello a me ritorna . . ." to end of stanza.

OROVESO and Chorus sing text from "ma irato, . . ." to end of that stanza.

NORMA:

(Ah! riedi ancora
qual eri allora,
quando, ah, quando il cor
ti diedi allora,
qual eri allora,
quando, ah, quando il cor ti diedi.
ah, riedi a me.)

(Ah! return again
to what you were then,
when, ah, when my heart
I gave to you then,
as you were then,
when, ah, when I gave you my heart.
ah, return to me.)

As NORMA sings last 3 lines above, OROVESO and Chorus sing:

O giorno, il Dio t'affretta
che il Tebro condannò.

O day, the god hastens you
whom the Tiber condemned.

—Felice Romani

Music drama - 3 acts   3 or 4 hours
intermission for Dinner

- wasn't until 1859 - score completed   - built out of themes   168
- originally intended as practical   or motifs
- ended up for his

girl

endless melody - avoides cadence   inner voice - chromatisism

156. TRISTAN UND ISOLDE, Prelude*
Richard Wagner (1813-1883)

that chord has had a book written about it. (Tristan chord)
opened up great harmonies

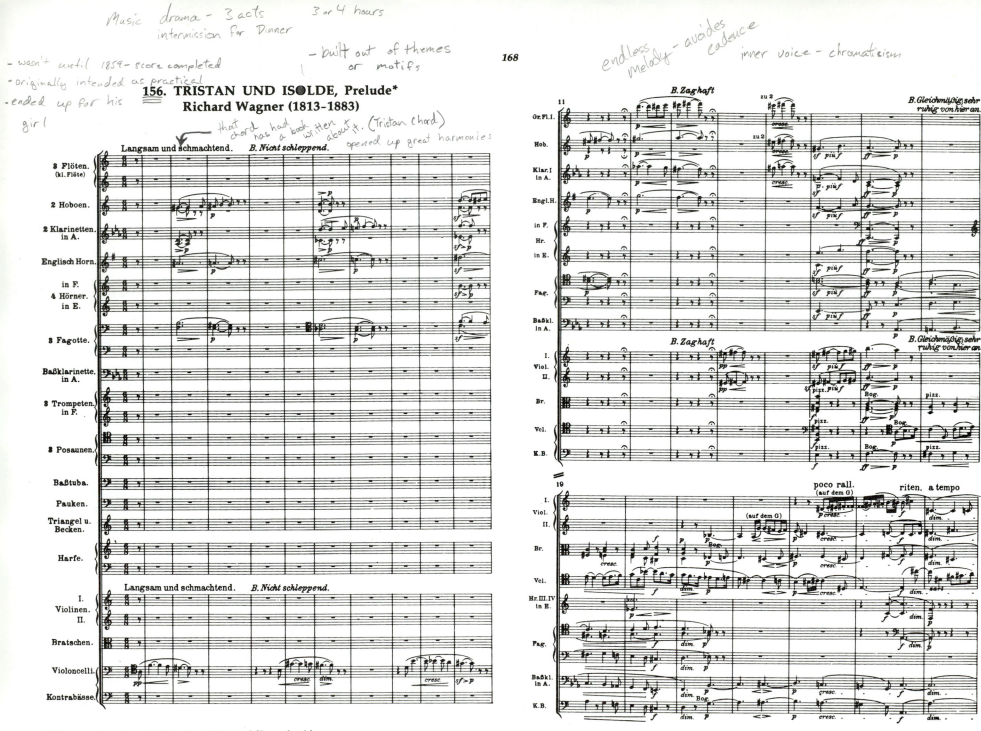

*Wagner referred to the Prelude as Liebestod (Love death).

Reprinted by permission of Dover Publications, Inc., Mineola, NY.

overall 3pt form

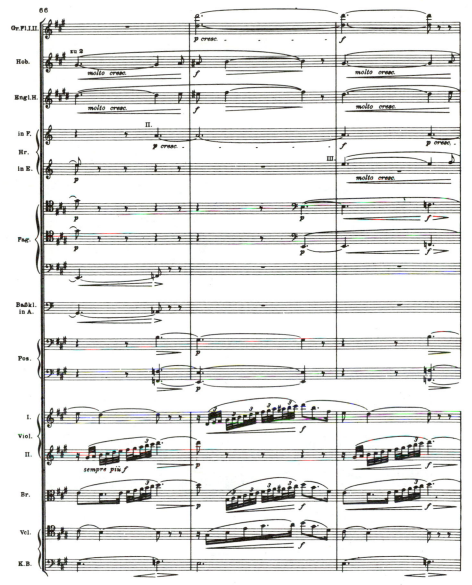

157. OTELLO, Act II, Scene 2
Giuseppe Verdi (1813–1901)

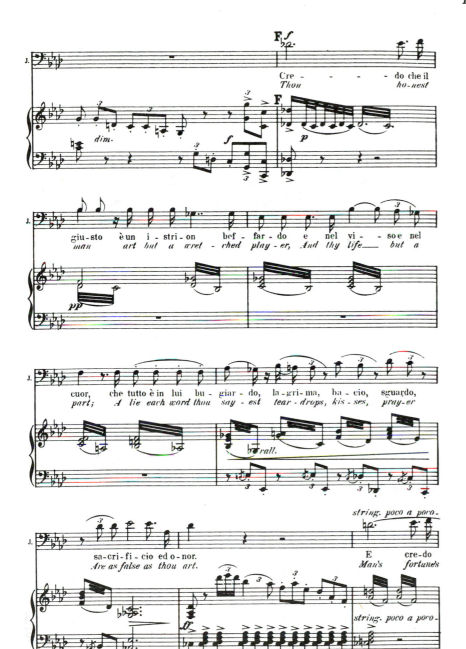

(Si vede passare nel giardino Desdemona con Emilia. Iago si slancia al verone, al di là del quale è appostato Cassio,
(*Desdemona and Emilia are seen to enter the garden. Iago goes toward the terrace beyond which*
Cassio has taken his position.)

(Cassio va verso Desdemona, la saluta, le s'accosta.)
(Cassio goes to Desdemona, bows to her and joins her.)

-sde-mo-na.
mo-na comes.

S'è
He's

mos-so;
near her;

la sa-lu-ta
And he greets her

e s'av-vi-
and does ac-

-ci-na.
cost her.

Or qui si tragga O-tel-lo!...
Now must I fetch O-thel-lo.

a-
Di-

-iu - - ta, a-iu-ta sà-ta-na il mio ci-men-to!...
vi - - ni-ties of hell I call u-pon your suc-cour!

Già con-ver - sa-no in-sie-me...
They are tal-king in whis-pers,

ed es-sa in-cli-na, sor-ri-den-do, il bel
and now To him has she in-clined her gent-le

(si vedono ripassare nel giardino Cassio e Desdemona)
(Cassio and Desdemona are seen passing backwards
and forwards in the garden.)

vi-so.
vi-sage.

Mi basta un lam-po
Ay, smile u-pon her

sol di quel sor-ri-
do! an excellent cour-te-

-so
syl

per
This

tra-sci-na-re O-tel-lo al-la ru-i-
smile shall lure O-thel-lo to his ru-

(fa per avviarsi rapido ma s'arresta subitamente)
(he goes rapidly towards the door but suddenly stops.)

-na.   An - diam...   Ma il
-in.   To - work!   and

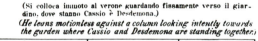

ca-so in mio fa-vor s'a - do-pra.   Ec - co - lo...   al
in this net I will en-slave him.   See, he comes,   good

(Si colloca immoto al verone guardando fissamente verso il giardino. dove stanno Cassio è Desdemona.)
(He leans motionless against a column looking intently towards
the garden where Cassio and Desdemona are standing together.)

po - sto,   al - l'o-pra.
luck!   I hace him.

(Jago solo seguendo coll' occhio Cassio.)

Vanne; la tua meta già vedo.
Ti spinge il tuo dimone,
e il tuo dimon son io,
e me trascina il mio, nel quale io credo
inesorato Iddio.

(Allontanandosi dal verone senza più
guarder Cassio che sarà scemparso
fra gli alberi.)

Credo in un Dio crudel che m'ha creato
simile a sè,

e che nell' ira io nomo.
Dalla viltà d'un germe o d'un atòmo vile
son nato.
Son scellerato perchè son uomo,
e sento il fango originario in me.
Sì! quest' è la mio fè!

Credo con fermo cor, siccome crede le
vedovella al tempio,
che il mal ch'io penso e che da me
precede
per mio destino adempio.

Credo che il giusto è un istrion beffardo
e nel viso e nel cuor;

che tutto è in lui bugiardo: lagrima,
bacio, sguardo, sacrificio ed onor.

E credo l'uom gioco d'iniqua sorte dal
germe della culla al verme dell' avel.

Vien dopo tanta irrision la Morte.
E poi? E poi? La Morte è il Nulla
è vecchia tola il Ciel.

(Iago alone, watching Cassio.)

Go on; your end assuredly [is] evil.
Your demon [or, genius] drives you,
and I am your demon,
and mine drives [or, impels] me,
the relentless God in whom I believe.

(Moving away from the balcony, no
longer looking at Cassio, who
disappears through the trees.)

I believe in a cruel God who has created
me like himself [= in his own
image],
and whom in wrath I call upon.
From the meanness of a germ or of a
contemptible atom I was born.
I am a villain because I am human,
and I feel the primal mud in me.
Yes! this is my creed!

I firmly believe, just as the widow
[praying] in the temple believes,
that the evil that I think and that
proceeds
from me is destined for me.

I believe that the honest man is a
scoffing actor both in his face and in
his heart;
that everything in him is falsehood:
tears, kisses, glances, sacrifice, and
honor.
And I believe man [is] the pawn of evil
fate from the cradle to the grave.
[literally, from the embryo in the womb
to the worm in the tomb.]

After so much mocking, death comes.
And then? And then? After death there
is nothing, and heaven is an old
woman's tale [or, an old wives' tale].

(Si vede passare nel giardino
Desdemona con Emilia. Jago si
slancia al verone, al di là del quale si
sarà appostato Cassio.)

(a Cassio)
Eccola . . . Cassio . . . a te . . .

Quest' è il momento.
Ti scuoti . . . vien Desdemona.

(Cassio va verso Desdemona, la saluta,
le s'accosta.)

S' è mosso; la saluta e s'avvicina.

Or qui si tragga Otello . . . !
aiuta, aiuta Satana il mio cimento . . . !

Già conversano insieme . . .
ed essa inclina, sorriendo, il bel viso.

Mi basta un lampo sol di quel sorriso
per trascinare Otello alla ruina.

Andiam . . .

(Fa per avviarsi rapide, ma i arresta
subitamente.)

Ma il caso in mio favor s'adopra.
Eccolo . . . al posto, all' opra.

(Si colloca immoto al verone, guardando
fissamente verso il giardino, dove
stanno Cassio e Desdemona.)

—A. Boito

(Desdemona is seen walking in the
garden with Emilia. Iago goes
quickly to the terrace beyond which
Cassio will be waiting.)

(to Cassio)
There she is . . . Cassio . . . for
you . . .
This is the moment.
Hurry . . . Desdemona comes.

(Cassio goes toward Desdemona, greets
her, joins her.)

He is near her; he greets her and
embraces her.
Now, if Otello is brought here . . . !
help, Satan, help my cause . . . !

Indeed, they are conversing . . .
and, smiling, she inclines her lovely
head.
For me, a single flash of such a smile is
sufficient to drag Otello to collapse
[= to break Otello's heart].
To work . . .

(He starts to walk rapidly, but stops
suddenly.)

But the situation is working in my favor.
Here he is . . . to the post [= get
ready], to work.

(He is motionless, leaning against a
column on the terrace, staring
intently toward the garden, where
Cassio and Desdemona are standing.)

158. LES JEUX D'EAUX À LA VILLA D'ESTE.
Franz Liszt (1811-1886)

*) Sed aqua quam ego dabo ei, fiet in eo fons aquae salientis in vitam aeternam (Evang. sec: Joannem 4-14.)

Translation: But the water that I shall give him, it shall be in him a well of water springing up unto life eternal. (John 4:14.)

159. NUAGES GRIS
Franz Liszt (1811–1886)

Permission by Edwin F. Kalmus & Company, Inc., Boca Raton, FL.

160. SYMPHONY NO. 3, Op. 90, mvt. 1
Johannes Brahms (1833–1897)

161. VIER ERNSTE GESÄNGE, Op. 121, No. 4
"Wenn ich mit Menschen und mit Engelzungen redete"
Johannes Brahms (1833–1897)

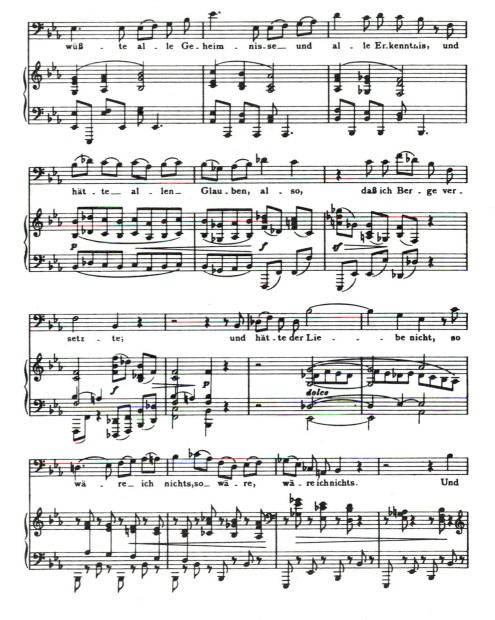

Wenn ich mit Menschen- und mit
Engel-zungen redete, und hätte Liebe
nicht, so wäre ich ein tönend Erz,
oder eine klingende Schelle.

If I speak with the tongues of men and
of angels, but have not love, I am
become sounding brass, or a clanging
cymbal.

Und wenn ich weissagen könnte, und wüsste alle Geheimnisse und alle Erkenntnis, und hätte allen Glauben, also, dass ich Berge versetzte, und hatte der Liebe nicht, so wäre ich nichts, so wäre, wäre ich nichts.

Und wenn ich alle meine Habe den Armen gäbe, und liesse meinen Leib brennen, meinen Leib brennen; und hätte der Liebe nicht, so wäre mir's nichts nütze, so wäre mir's nichts nütze.

Wir sehen jetzt durch einen Spiegel in einem dunkeln Worte, dann aber von Angesicht zu Angesichte.

Jetzt erkenne ich's stuckweise, dann aber werd ich's erkennen, gleich wie ich erkennet bin.

Nun aber bleibet Glaube, Hoffnung, Liebe, diese drei; aber die Liebe ist die grosseste unter ihnen, die Liebe ist die grosseste unter ihnen.
—Die Bibel (The Bible), (1874)
I Corinther 13:1–3; 12,13.

And if I have the gift of prophecy and know all mysteries and all knowledge, and have all faith, so as to move mountains, but have not love, I am nothing.

And if I bestow all my goods on the poor, and if I give my body to be burned; and have not love, it profiteth me nothing.

Now we see in a mirror, darkly; but then face to face.

Now I know in part, but then I shall know fully, even as also I was fully known.

But now abideth faith, hope, love, these three; but the greatest of these is Love.

—The Holy Bible,
(Standard edition, 1901)
I Corinthians 13:1–3; 12,13.

162. VIRGA JESSE FLORUIT, Motet
Anton Bruckner (1824–1896)

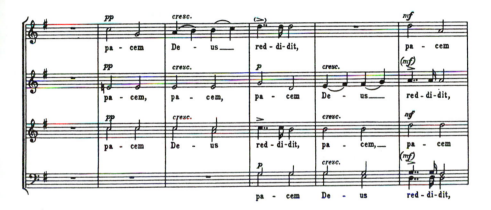

Virga Jesse floruit:
Virgo Deum et hominem genuit:

pacem Deus reddidit,
in se reconcilians ima summis.

Alleluja.

The rod of Jesse blossomed:
A virgin brought forth [both] God and
  man:
God restored peace,
in Himself reconciling the lowest [and]
  highest.

Alleluia.

163. BORIS GODUNOV, Prologue, Scene 2: Coronation Scene
Modest Musorgsky (1839–1881)

Площадь в Кремле московском. Прямо перед зрителями, в отдалении, Красное крыльцо царских теремов. Справа, ближе к авансцене, народ на коленях занимает место между Успенским и Архангельским соборами: паперти соборов видны

A square in the Moscow Kremlin. Facing the audience, up-stage, the Great Staircase of the Imperial Palace. Right, down-stage, the crowd is kneeling in the space between the Cathedral of the Assumption and the Cathedral of the Archangels. The porches of both cathedrals are visible.

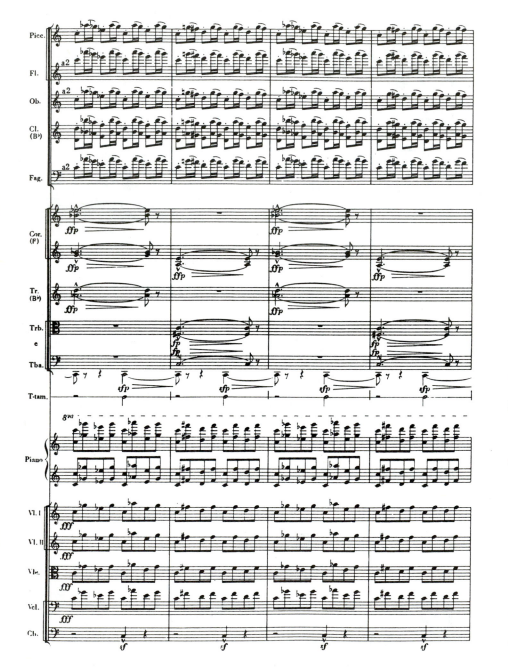

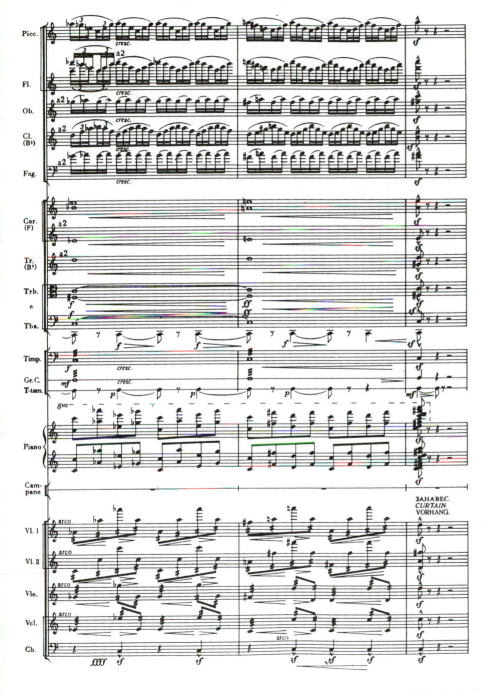

Великий колокольный звон на сцене
A great peal of bells on stage.

С Красного крыльца начинается торжественное шествие бояр к Успенскому собору: впереди рынды, стрельцы, боярские дети; далее князь Шуйский с венцом Мономаха на падушке; за ним бояре. Щелкалов с царским посохом, н.т.д...

From the Great Staircase boyars in solemn procession start towards the Cathedral of the Assumption; in front are guards, Streltsy, and boyar children; then comes Shuisky, carrying the crown of Monomach on a cushion. Behind him boyars, Shchelkalov carrying the Imperial sceptre, etc.

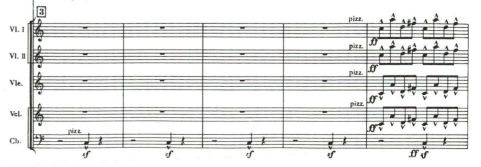

213

218

219

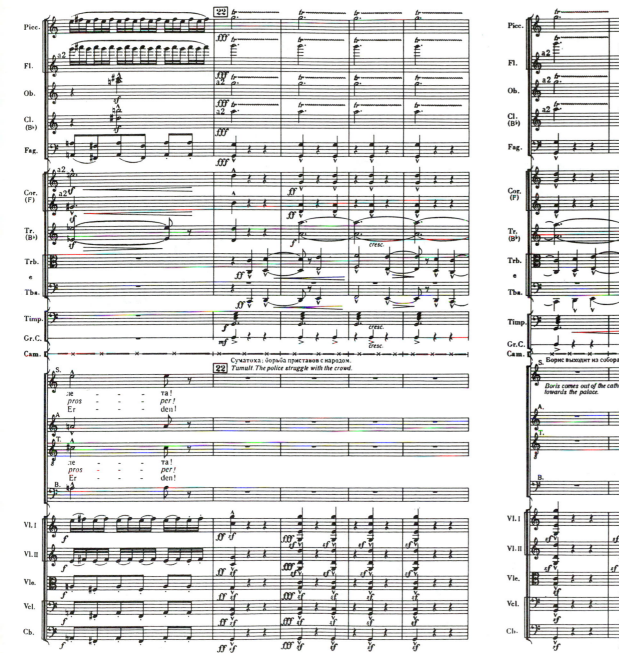

164. PRELUDE, Op. 74, No. 3
Alexander Scriabin (1872–1915)

Allegro drammatico

165. ANAKREONS GRAB, Lied
Hugo Wolf (1860–1903)

Sehr langsam und ruhig
(*Very slowly and calmly*)

Wo die Ro-se hier blüht, ___ wo Re-ben und Lor-beer sich schlin-gen, wo das Tur-tel-chen lockt. ___ wo sich das Grill-chen er-götzt, ___ welch ein Grab ist hier, das ___ al- le Göt-ter mit Le- - - ben schön be-pflanzt und ge-

Wo die Rose hier blüht,
wo Reben und Lorbeer sich schlingen,
wo das Turtelchen lockt,
wo sich das Grillchen ergötzt,
welch ein Grab ist hier,
das alle Götter mit Leben
schön bepflanzt und geziert?

Es ist Anakreons Ruh.
Frühling, Sommer und Herbst
genoss der glückliche Dichter.
Vor dem Winter hat ihn endlich
der Hügel geschützt.

—J. W. von Goethe

Here where the rose blooms,
where vines and laurel entwine,
where the turtledove coos,
where the little cricket enjoys itself,
whose grave is here,
that all the gods
beautifully planted and adorned with
life?

It is Anakreon's resting place.
Spring, summer, and winter
the happy poet enjoyed.
Finally, from the winter
the mound has protected him.

166. KINDERTOTENLIEDER: No. 5, "In diesem Wetter, in diesem Braus" Gustav Mahler (1860–1911)

In diesem Wetter, in diesem Braus,
Nie hätt' ich gesendet die Kinder
    hinaus!
Man hat sie hinaus getragen!
Ich durfte nichts dazu sagen!

In diesem Wetter, in diesem Saus,
Nie hätt' ich gelassen die Kinder hinaus,

Ich fürchtete, sie erkranken;
Das sind nun eitle Gedanken.

In diesem Wetter, in diesem Graus,
Nie hätt' ich gelassen die Kinder hinaus.

Ich sorgte, sie stürben morgen;

Das ist nun nicht zu besorgen.

In diesem Wetter, in diesem Graus,
Nie hätt' ich gesendet die Kinder
    hinaus,
Man hat sie hinaus getragen,
Ich durfte nichts dazu sagen!

In diesem Wetter, in diesem Saus,
In diesem Braus, sie ruh'n, sie ruh'n
Als wie in der Mutter, der Mutter Haus;

Von keinem Sturm erschrekket,
Von Gottes Hand bedekket,
Sie ruh'n, sie ruh'n in der Mutter Haus!

—Friedrich Rückert

In this weather, in this storm,
I would never have sent the children out!

They have been carried out!
I was not permitted to say anything
    about it!

In this weather, in this storm,
I would never have permitted the
    children out,
I was afraid they might become ill;
These are now idle thoughts.

In this weather, in this dreadfulness,
I would never have permitted the
    children out.
I was afraid they might die on the
    morrow,
That is no longer to be dreaded.

In this weather, in this dreadfulness,
I would never have sent the children out,

They have been carried out,
I had nothing to say about it!

In this weather, in this storm,
In this tumult, they rest, they rest
As though in their mother's, their
    mother's house;
By no storm frightened,
By God's hand protected,
They rest, they rest as though in their
    mother's house!

167. LA BONNE CHANSON: No. 9, "L'Hiver a cessé"
Gabriel Fauré (1845-1924)

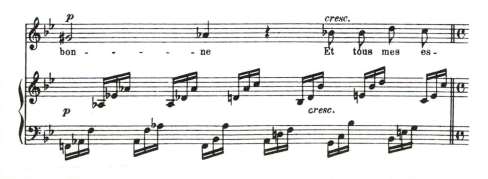

ron - ne L'im-mu-able a-zur où rit mon a-

-poirs ont en-fin leur tour. Que

-mour. La sai-son est

vien - ne l'é-té que vien-nent en-

bel - le et ma part est

-co - re l'au-tom-ne et l'hi-ver! Et

bon - ne Et tous mes es-

cha - que sai-son me se-ra char-man -

L'Hiver a cessé, la lumière est tiède
Et danse, du sol au firmament clair,

Il faut que le coeur le plus triste cède
À l'immense joie éparse dans l'air.
J'ai depuis un an le printemps dans
l'âme,
Et le vert retour du doux floréal,

Ainsi qu'une flamme entoure une
flamme,
Met de l'idéal sur mon idéal.
Le ciel bleu prolonge, exhausse et
couronne
L'immuable azur où rit mon amour.

La saison est belle et ma part est bonne,

Et tous mes espoirs ont enfin leur tour.
Que vienne l'Été! Que viennent encore
L'Automne et l'Hiver! Et chaque saison
Me sera charmante, ô toi, que décore
Cette fantaisie et cette raison!

—Paul Verlaine

Winter is over, the light is soft
And dances from the earth to the clear
sky;
The saddest heart must now give way
To the great joy scattered in the air.
For a whole year I have had spring in
my soul,
And the green return of sweet blossom
time,
Like a flame surrounding a flame,

Adds ideals to my ideal.
The blue sky extends, heightens and
crowns
The unchangeable azure, where my love
rejoices.
The season is lovely and my share is
good,
And all my hopes at last have their day.
Let Summer come! Let also come
Autumn and Winter! And every season
For me will be lovely, oh you, whom
This fantasy and this thought adorn!

English translation by Waldo Lyman

168. PRÉLUDE À L'APRÈS-MIDI D'UN FAUNE
Claude Debussy (1862–1918)

257

261

169. JEUX D'EAU
Maurice Ravel (1875–1937)

Permission by Edwin F. Kalmus & Company, Inc., Boca Raton, FL.

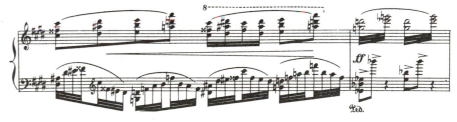

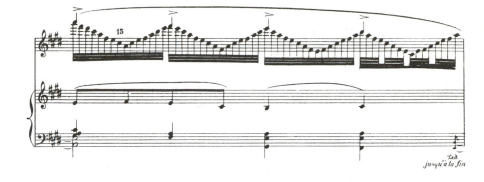

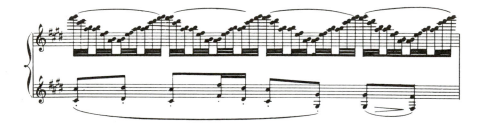

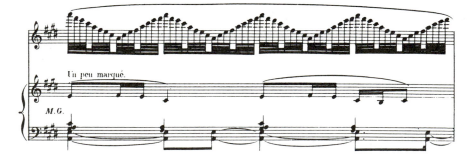

hidden blurred
Cadance
V - I

170. THE HYMN OF JESUS
Gustav Holst (1874–1934)

PRELUDE.

Source: Galaxy Music Corporation, Boston, MA.

HYMN.

*Beginning of recorded excerpt.

277

16
Poco più mosso.
For yours is the pas - sion of man that I go to en - dure.
dim.
p
cresc.
pp
17 Trebles only of both Choruses and Semi-chorus.
Ah Ah Ah Ah Ah Ah
Ah Ah
con Ped.
(dim.)
dim
Largo.
f
mp
18
pp
Ye could not know at all
Ye could not know at all
Ye could not know at
Ye could not know
Coll 8
What thing ye en - dure, had not the Fa - ther sent me to you as a
know at all
could not know at all
at all

*Conclusion of recorded excerpt.

171. SECOND PIANO SONATA: "Concord, Mass., 1840–1860," mvt. 3: "The Alcotts"
Charles Ives (1874–1954)

"The Alcotts" from SECOND PIANO SONATA by Charles Ives. Copyright © 1947, 1976 (Renewed), by Associated Music Publishers, Inc. (BMI) International Copyright Secured. All Rights Reserved. Used By Permission.

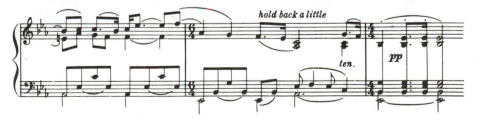

172. THE BANSHEE
Henry Cowell (1897-1965)

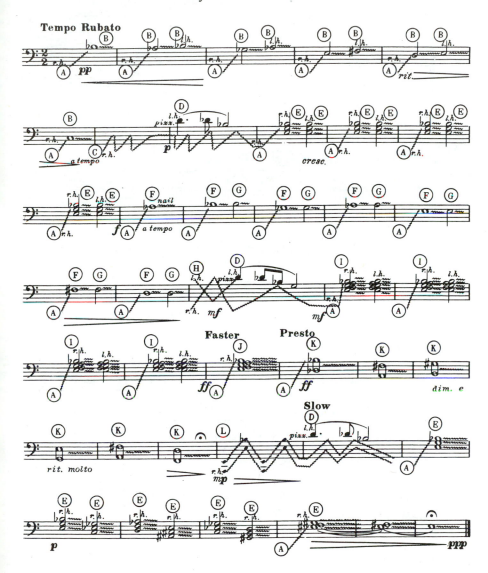

Explanation of Symbols

"The Banshee" is played on the open strings of the piano, the player standing at the crook. Another person must sit at the keyboard and hold down the damper pedal throughout the composition. The whole work should be played an octave lower than written.

R. H. stands for "right hand." L. H. stands for "left hand." Different ways of playing the strings are indicated by a letter over each tone, as follows:

(A) indicates a sweep with the flesh of the finger from the lowest string up to the note given.

(B) sweep lengthwise along the string of the note given with flesh of finger.

(C) sweep up and back from lowest A to highest B-flat given in this composition.

(D) pluck string with flesh of finger, where written, instead of octave lower.

(E) sweep along three notes together, in the same manner as (B).

(F) sweep in the manner of (B) but with the back of finger-nail instead of flesh.

(G) when the finger is half way along the string in the manner of (F), start a sweep along the same string with the flesh of the other finger, thus partly damping the sound.

(H) sweep back and forth in the manner of (C), but start at the same time from both above and below, crossing the sweep in the middle.

(I) sweep along five notes, in the manner of (B).

(J) same as (I) but with back of finger-nails instead of flesh of finger.

(K) sweep along in manner of (J) with nails of both hands together, taking in all notes between the two outer limits given.

(L) sweep in manner of (C) with flat of hand instead of single finger.

173. MUSIC FOR STRINGS, PERCUSSION, AND CELESTA, mvt. 1
Béla Bartók (1882–1945)

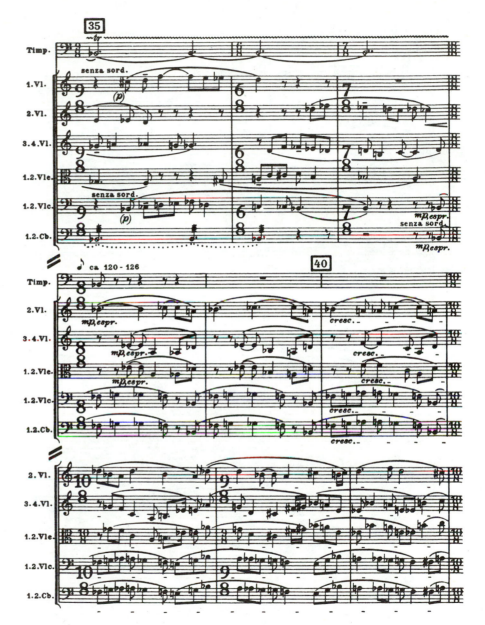

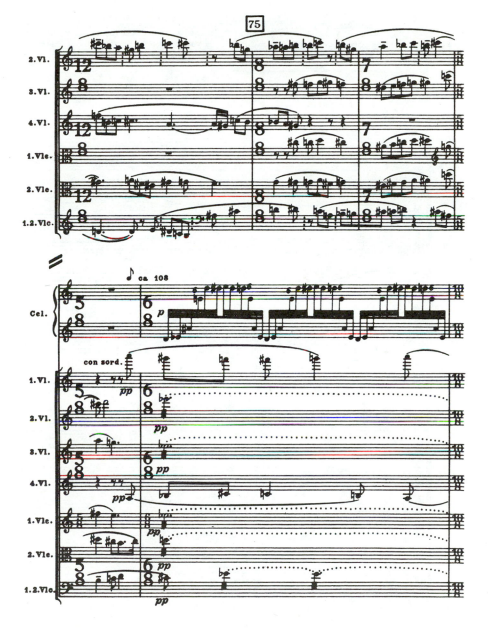

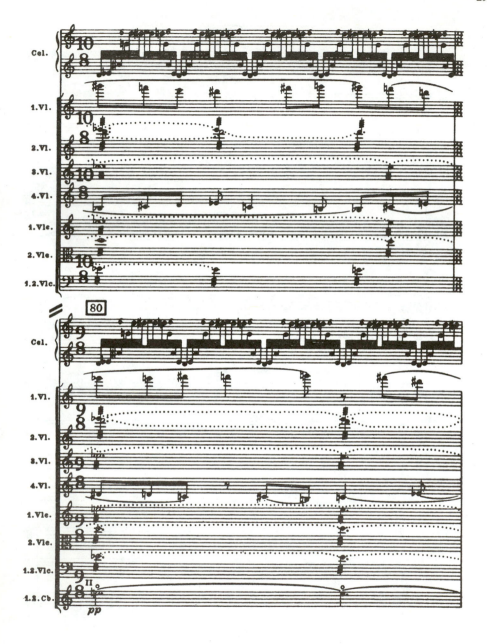

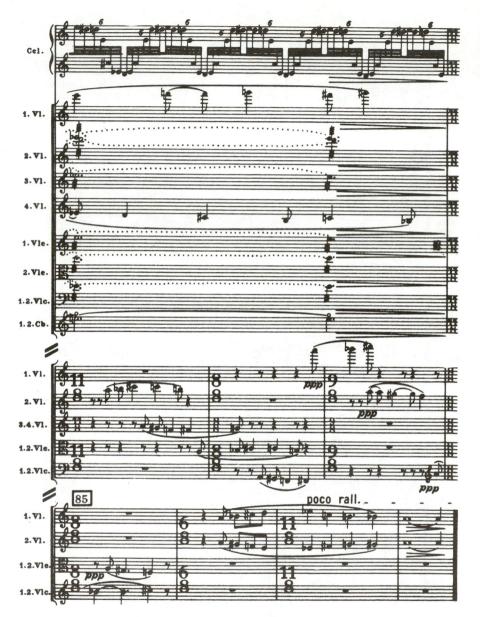

- tonality based on a single
  pitch.-

Ending on same
pitch he started with

174. PIERROT LUNAIRE, Excerpts
Arnold Schoenberg (1874–1951)

a. No. 8, Nacht

Finistre, schwarze Riesenfalter	Sinister, black, giant butterflies
Tötenten der Sonne Glanz.	Eclipse the splendor of the sun.
Ein geschlossnes Zauberbuch	A sealed conjuring book,
Ruht der Horizont—verschwiegen.	The horizon sleeps—silent.
Aus dem Qualm verlorner Tiefnen	Out of the dense vapor of the forgotten depths
Steigt ein Duft, Erinnerung mordend!	Rises a perfume, murdering memory!
Finistre, schwarze Riesenfalter	Sinister, black, giant butterflies
Tötenten der Sonne Glanz.	Eclipse the splendor of the sun.
Und von Himmel erdenwarts	And from heaven, earthward
Senken sich mit schweren Schwingen	Sinking with heavy wings,
Unsichtbar die Ungetüme	Invisible, the monsters
Auf die Menschenherzen nieder . . .	Descend upon men's hearts . . .
Finistre, schwarze Riesenfalter.	Sinister, black, giant butterflies.

—German translation of original French
is by Otto Erich Hartleben

b. No. 18, Der Mondfleck

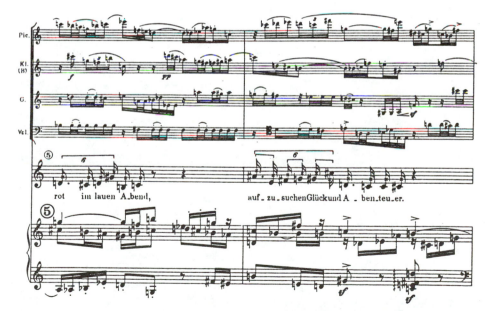

Plötzlich stört ihn was an sei_nem An _ zug, er be_

des hel_len Mon _ _ des auf dem Rük_ken sei_nes schwarzen Rockes. War_te!

sieht sich rings und fin_det rich_tig_ ei_nen wei_ßen Fleck

denkt er: das ist so ein Gips _ fleck! Wischt und wischt, doch

Einen weissen Fleck des hellen Mondes	A white spot of bright moonlight
Auf dem Rücken seines schwarzen Rockes,	On the back of his black jacket,
So spaziert Pierrot im lauen Abend,	Pierrot strolls about in the mild evening,
Aufzusuchen Glück und Abenteuer.	To search for good fortune and adventure.
Plötzlich stört ihn was an seinem Anzug,	Suddenly, something about his clothing bothers him,
Er beschaut sich rings und findet richtig—	He inspects himself and, indeed, finds—
Einen weissen Fleck des hellen Mondes	A white spot of bright moonlight
Auf dem Rücken seines schwarzen Rockes.	On the back of his black jacket.
Warte! denkt er: das ist so ein Gipsfleck!	Wait! he thinks: that is a fleck of gypsum!
Wischt und wischt, doch— bringt ihn nicht herunter!	He wipes and wipes, still— he can't get rid of it!
Und so geht er, giftgeschwollen, weiter, Reibt und reibt bis an den frühen Morgen—	And so he goes on, filled with venom, He rubs and rubs until dawn—
Einen weissen Fleck des hellen Mondes.	A white spot of bright moonlight.

—German translation of original French is by Otto Erich Hartleben

12-tone Method

175. VARIATIONEN FÜR ORCHESTER, Op. 31, Excerpts
Arnold Schoenberg (1874–1951)

a. Introduction, Thema

b. Finale

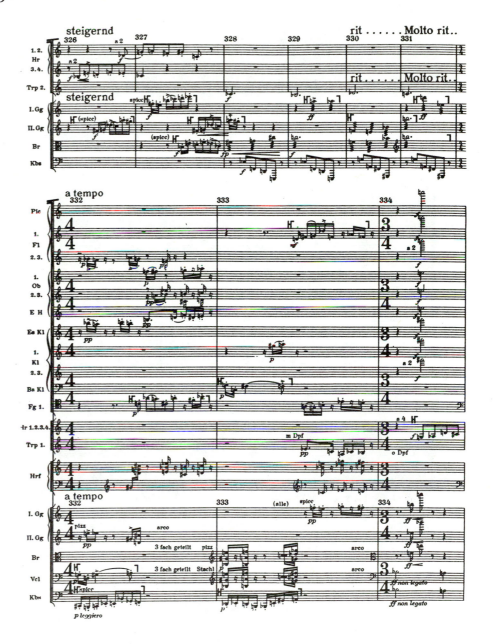

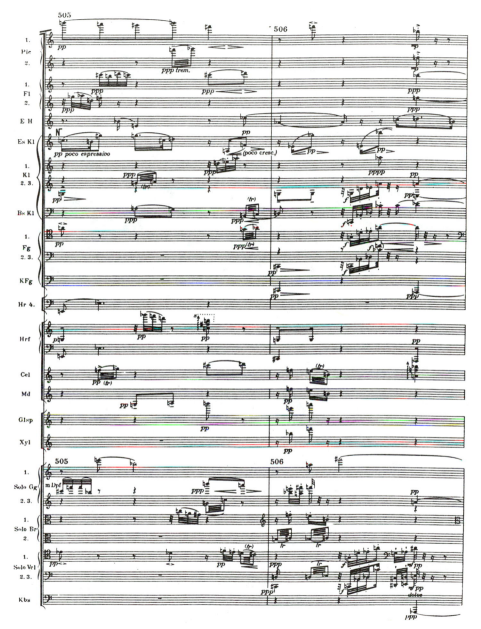

176. WOZZECK, Act III, Scene 2
Alban Berg (1885–1936)

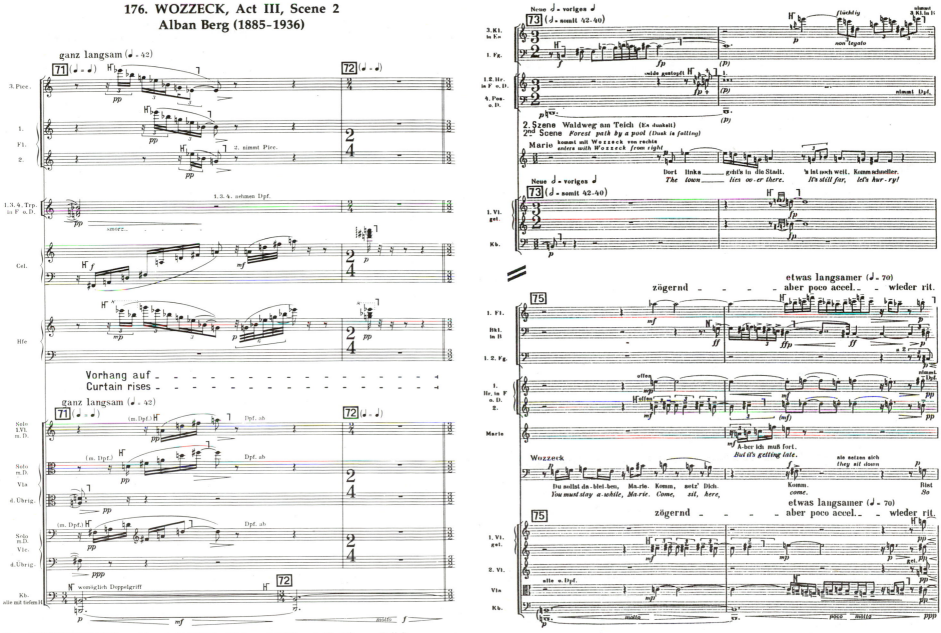

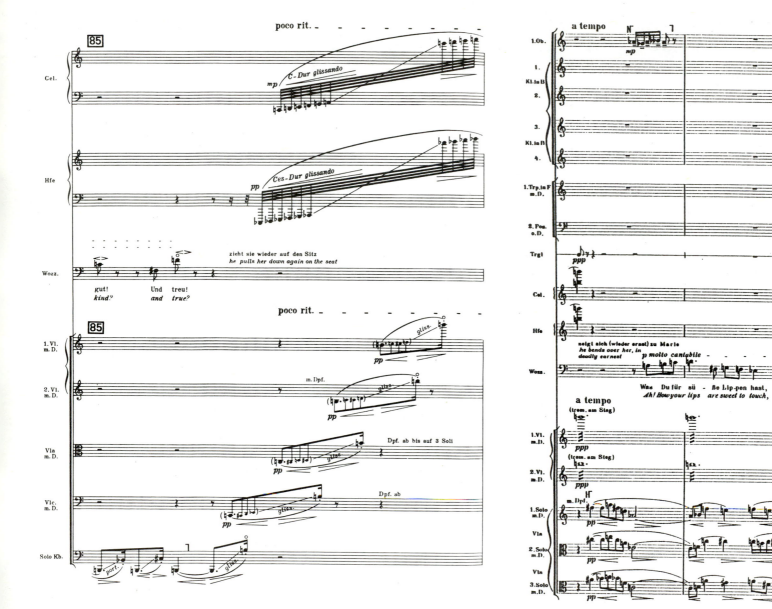

320

177. SYMPHONIE, Op. 21, mvt. 2 excerpts
Anton Webern (1883–1945)

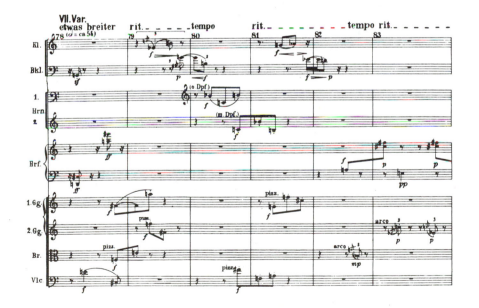

178. LE SACRE DU PRINTEMPS, Part 1, Adoration of the Earth: Introduction, The Augurs of Spring—Dances of the Young Girls
Igor Stravinsky (1882-1971)

THE AUGURS OF SPRING
DANCES OF THE YOUNG GIRLS
LES AUGURES PRINTANIERS
DANSES DES ADOLESCENTES

29
Fl. picc.
Fl. gr.
Fl. alto
Ob.
Cl. picc. in Mib
Cl. in Sib
Cl. bas. in Sib
Fag.
C. Fag.
Tr. in Do
Trbn.
Timp.
Triang.
Cym. ant.
Vl. I
Vl. II div.
Vle. div. a3
3 Soli Vc. gli altri
Cb
mf
f stacc.
mp cantab.
bacch. di legno
legg. 5.6 f
legg 7.8 f
Tutti div.
arco
marcatiss. e molto cantabile
C. ing.
Cor. in Fa
sim.
C. ing. 2 muta in Ob 4
Fag. 4 muta in C. Fag. 2
Vl. I div.

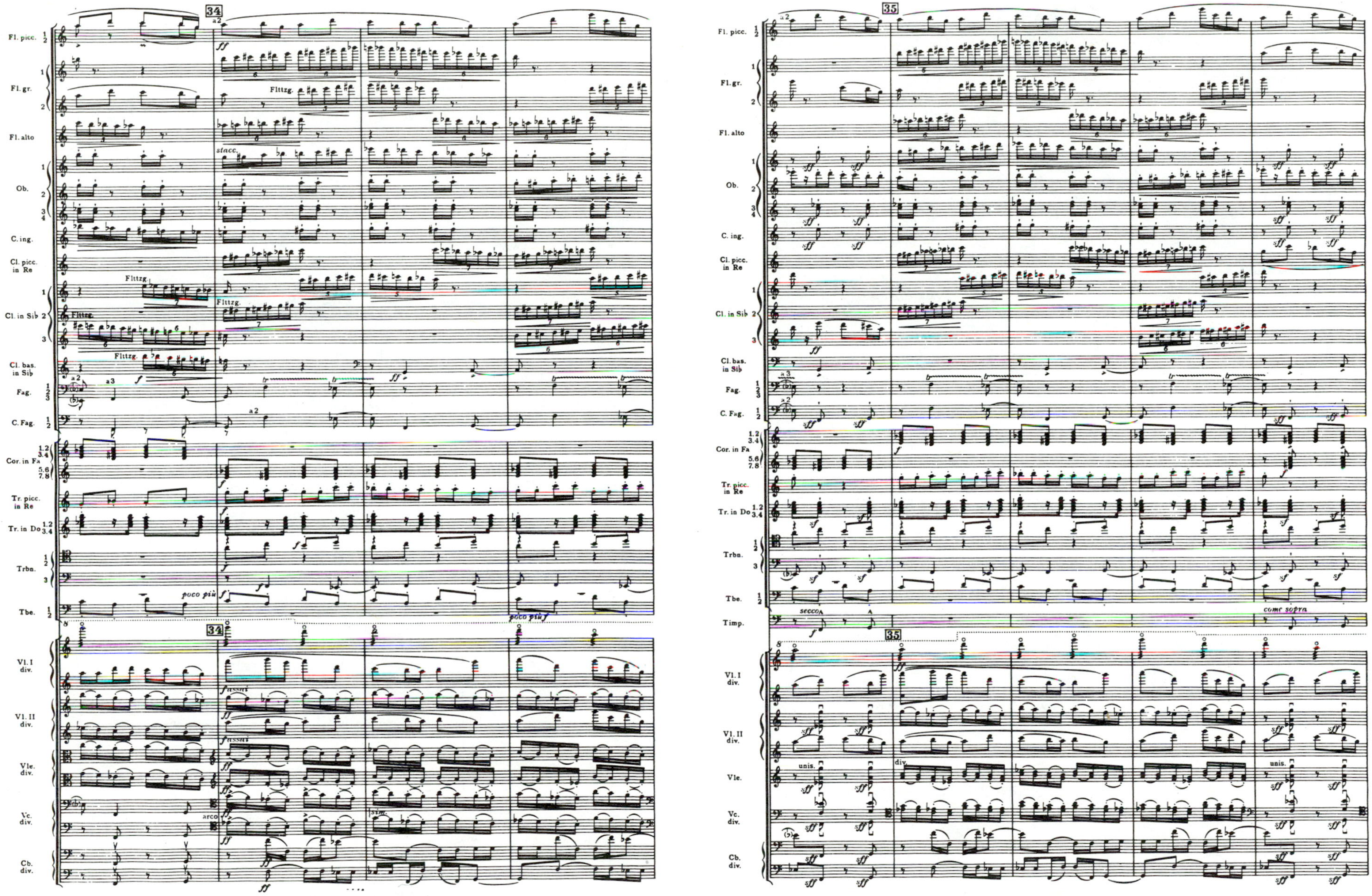
34
35
Fl. picc.
Fl. gr.
Fl. alto
Ob.
C. ing.
Cl. picc. in Re
Cl. in Sib
Cl. bas. in Sib
Fag.
C. Fag.
Cor. in Fa
Tr. picc. in Re
Tr. in Do
Trbn.
Tbe.
Timp.
Vl. I div.
Vl. II div.
Vle. div.
Vle.
Vc. div.
Cb. div.
Flttzg.
stacc.
poco più
poco più f
fassai
arco
sim.
secco
come sopra
unis.
div.

179. SYMPHONY OF PSALMS, mvt. 2
Igor Stravinsky (1882–1971)

Expectans expectavi DOMINUM,
et intendit mihi.
Et exaudivit preces meas:
et eduxit me de lacu miseriae, et de
luto faecis.

Expectantly, I waited for the Lord,
and He was attentive to me.
And He heard my prayers;
and He brought me up out of the pit
of wretchedness, and out of the miry
clay.

Et statuit super petram pedes meos:
et direxit gressus meos.
Et immisit in os meum canticum novum,
carmen DEO nostro.
Videbunt multi, et timebunt:
et sperabunt in DOMINO.

—*Biblia sacra*, Psalmus XXXIX: 2–4.
(Vulgate)

And He set my feet upon a rock;
and He directed my steps.
And He put a new song in my mouth,
a hymn to our God.
Many shall see and shall fear;
and they shall hope in the Lord.

—*The Holy Bible*, Psalm 39: 2–4
Vulgate; Psalm 40: 1–3 KJV

180. APPALACHIAN SPRING, Section 7
Aaron Copland (1900-90)

* Shaker melody "The gift to be simple"

347

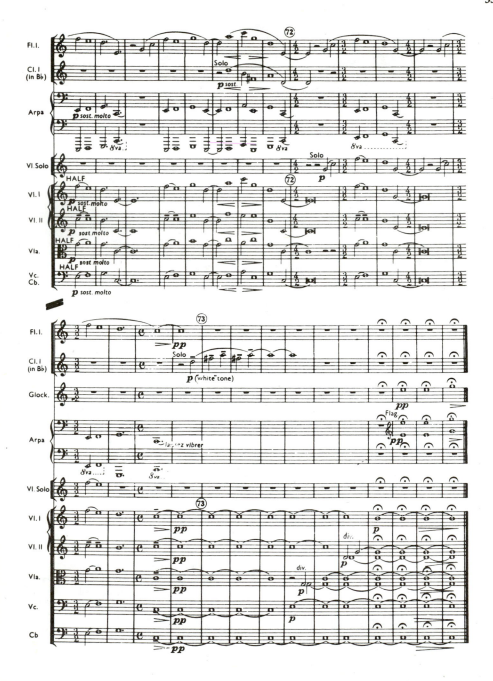

350

181. MÉDITATIONS SUR LE MYSTÈRE DE LA SAINTE TRINITÉ, No. VII

Olivier Messiaen (1908-92)

In three parts: Introduction—Body of the piece in "communicable language"—Coda. *Introduction.* . . . [includes] the song of an unknown bird. I heard this bird at Persepolis, in Iran, one evening at sunset. . . . I notated his song. . . . Not having seen the bird, and hearing his magnificent song for the first time, I called it: "bird of Persepolis." There follows the effect of four horns that fade away. . . . *Body of the piece.* It is written as a trio, on the Positif, the Pedals, the Récit. . . . On the Récit, on trumpet 8 and bourdon 16, middle voice: it is written in "communicable language." The words translated are drawn from this text of Saint Thomas Aquinas: "The Father and the Son love, *through the Holy Spirit* (the Love that proceeds), themselves and us." (Somme Théologique—"the Trinity," volume II—question 37, article 2, conclusion). This gives musically: Père (theme for the Father), Fils (the same theme in contrary motion, as two glances that cross)—aiment (theme for the verb aimer [to love])—Père, Fils, (ablatif: par [ablative case: through]) Saint Esprit (theme for God original and retrograde)—Amour (the verb aimer [to love]). Father, Son—love—the human race—through the Holy Spirit—the Love, of the Father, of the Son. *Coda.* We take again the seven chords of the Introduction, in forward motion, then in retrograde motion. New strophe of "bird of Persepolis." The effect of the four horns that fade away brings [tonality] to the dominant—then, it concludes on the tonic E major, solemnly and distantly.

—O. Messiaen

The "communicable language" series:

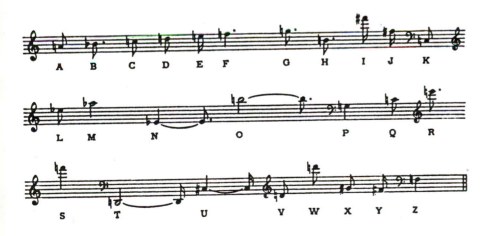

Comb. 5

R: trompette 8 et bourdon 16 <|
Pos: quintaton 16, flûte 4, nazard 2 ⅔,
     piccolo 1 <|
Ped: sb. 16, bourdon 8, flûte 4 −|

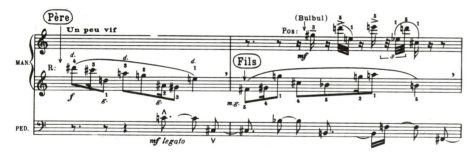

353

MAN. (Amour – verbe aimer)

PED.

MAN. Fils

PED.

MAN. p r o c é

PED.

MAN. (aiment – verbe aimer)

PED.

MAN. d a n t

PED.

MAN. r a c e h u

PED.

MAN. Père

PED.

MAN. m a i n e

PED.

(ablatif: par)

Père

Saint Esprit

(génitif: du)

Fils

(Amour – verbe aimer)

Comb. 3

R: bourdon 16, bourdon 8, nazard 2 ⅔, octavin 2, 3ᶜᵉ 1 ⅗ – ▷ |
Pos: quintaton 16, fourniture 4 rangs, piccolo 1 – ◁ |
G: bourdon 16, montre 8, fl. harm., bourdon 8 – | Ped: sb. 32, sb. 16, bourdon 8 – tir. R | ⟶

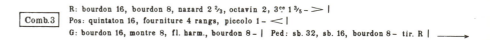

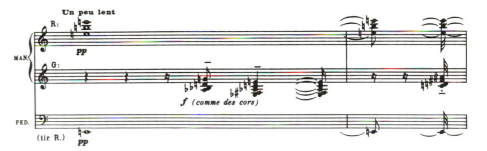

(oiseau de Persépolis)

"Le Père et le Fils aiment, par le Saint-Esprit (l'Amour qui procède), eux-mêmes, et nous."

(Saint Thomas d'Aquin, Somme Théologique – "la Trinité", tome II – question 37, article 2, conclusion –)

182. LE MARTEAU SANS MAÎTRE, mvt. 3: "l'artisanat furieux"
Pierre Boulez (b. 1925)

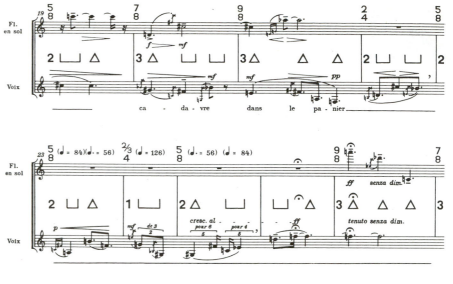

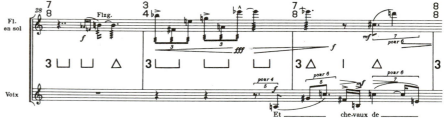

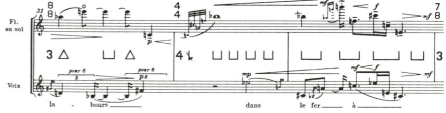

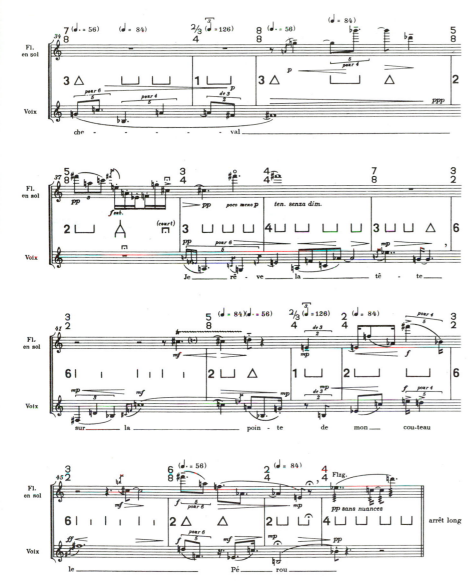

183. THREE COMPOSITIONS FOR PIANO, No. 1
Milton Babbitt (b. 1916)

I

Accidentals affect only those notes which they immediately precede, except when notes are tied

The sign ⌐ ¬ denotes the duration of *una corda*.

The following tempi may be substituted for those indicated in the first and third compositions: 96 instead of 108, and 112 instead of 126.

© Copyright 1957 by Boelke-Bomart, Inc.; used by permission.

La roulotte rouge au bord du clou

Et cadavre dans le panier
Et chevaux de labours dans le fer à
    cheval
Je rêve, la tête sur la pointe de mon
    couteau, le Pérou.

—René Char

The red caravan at the edge of the
    prison
And a corpse in the basket
And a workhorse in the horseshoe

I dream, head on the point of my knife,
    Peru.

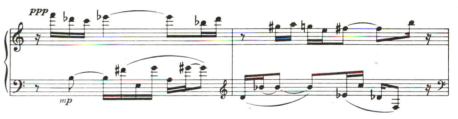

184. ANCIENT VOICES OF CHILDREN: I, "El niño busca su voz"
George Crumb (b. 1929)

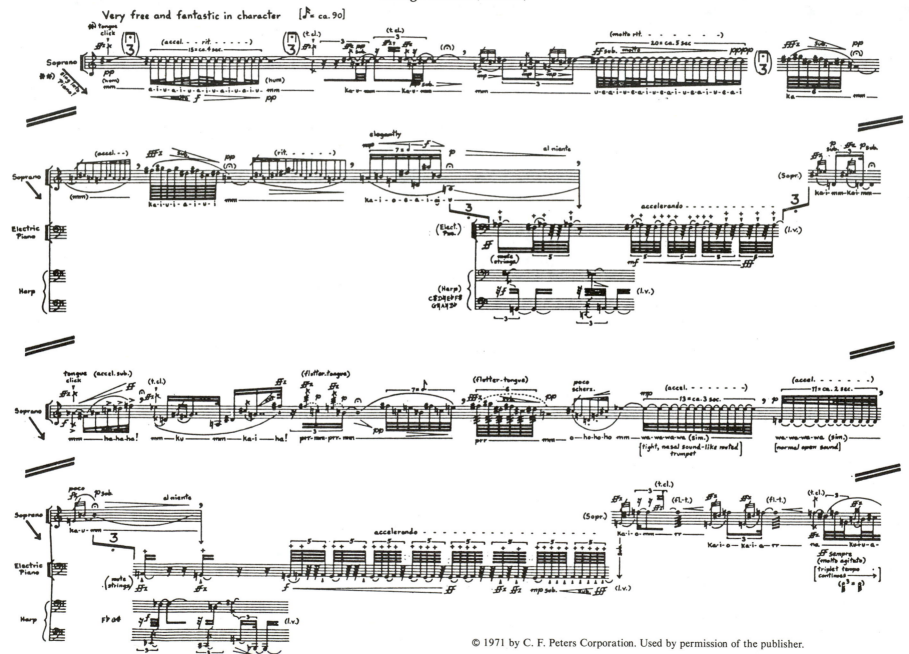

361

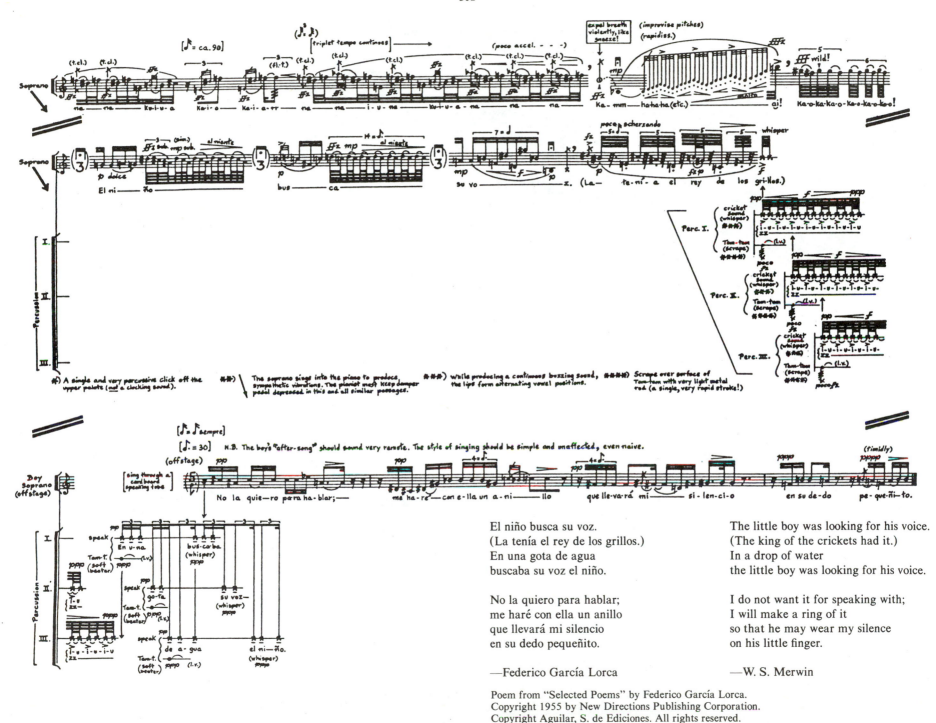

El niño busca su voz.
(La tenía el rey de los grillos.)
En una gota de agua
buscaba su voz el niño.

No la quiero para hablar;
me haré con ella un anillo
que llevará mi silencio
en su dedo pequeñito.

—Federico García Lorca

The little boy was looking for his voice.
(The king of the crickets had it.)
In a drop of water
the little boy was looking for his voice.

I do not want it for speaking with;
I will make a ring of it
so that he may wear my silence
on his little finger.

—W. S. Merwin

Poem from "Selected Poems" by Federico García Lorca.
Copyright 1955 by New Directions Publishing Corporation.
Copyright Aguilar, S. de Ediciones. All rights reserved.

185. APPARITION: I. "The night in silence under many a star . . ."
George Crumb (b. 1929)

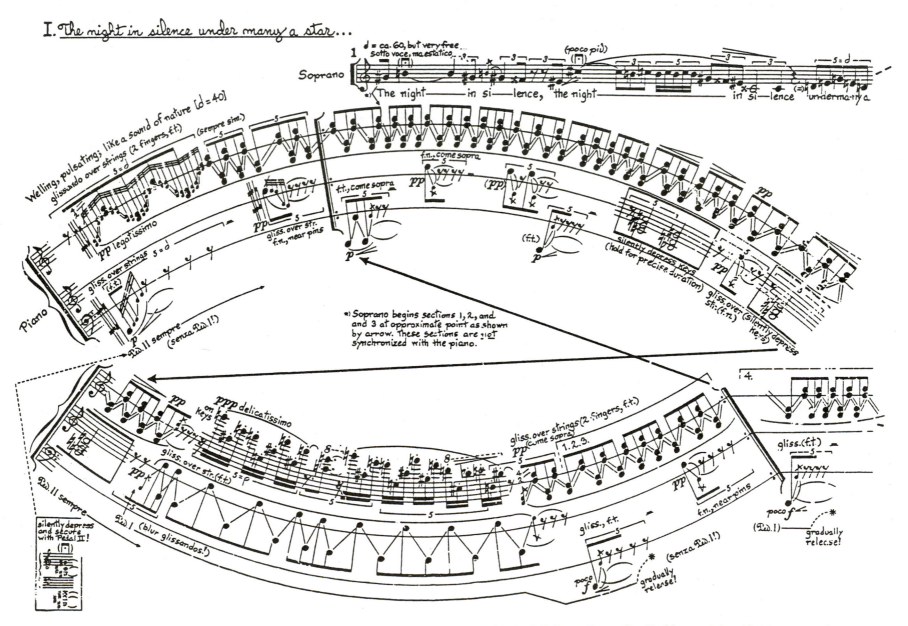

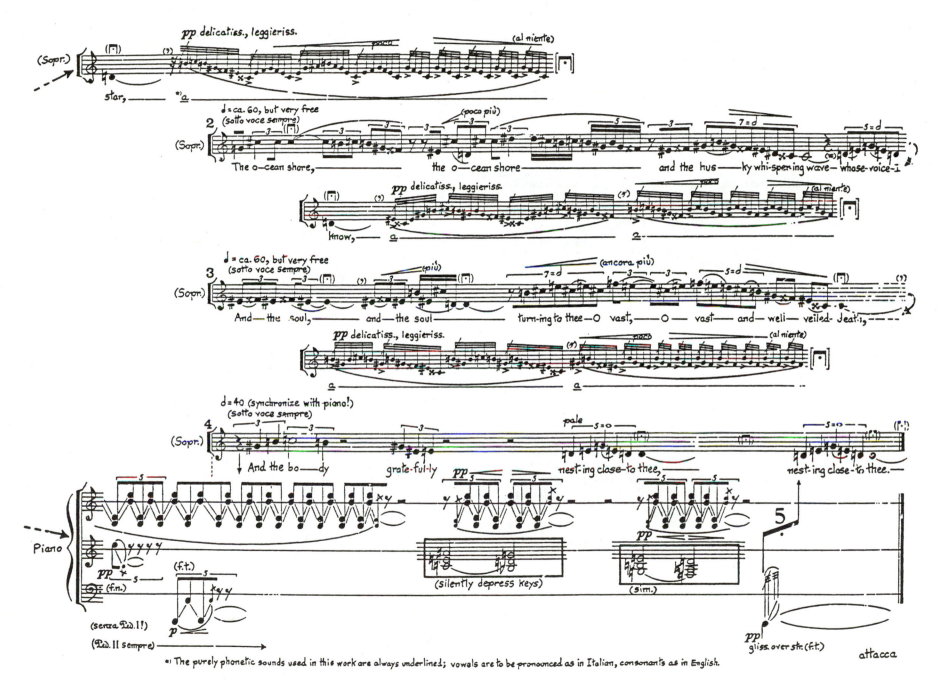

*) The purely phonetic sounds used in this work are always underlined; vowels are to be pronounced as in Italian, consonants as in English.

attacca

186. ÉJSZAKA/NIGHT
György Ligeti (b. 1929)

187. TEHILLIM (Psalms): Part IV
Steve Reich (b. 1936)

INSTRUMENTATION

Piccolo*

Flute* (1, 2, 3)

Oboe* (1, 2)

English Horn*

Clarinets in B♭ 1*, 2*, (3, 4)

(Bassoon)

Percussion –6 Players

Maracas

Clapping

Tuned tambourines without jingles	Part I 1, 2, 3, 4 (A, G, E, D)	Part II 1, 2 (A♭, E♭)
	Part III Tacent	Part IV 1, 2 (A, E)

Marimba

Vibraphone

Crotales

Electric organ 1, 2

Women's voices   1, Lyric Soprano*
                  2, Lyric Soprano*
                  3, Alto*
                  4, High Soprano*

Strings—solo* (section)

*Amplified
( ) Parentheses = full orchestral version additions

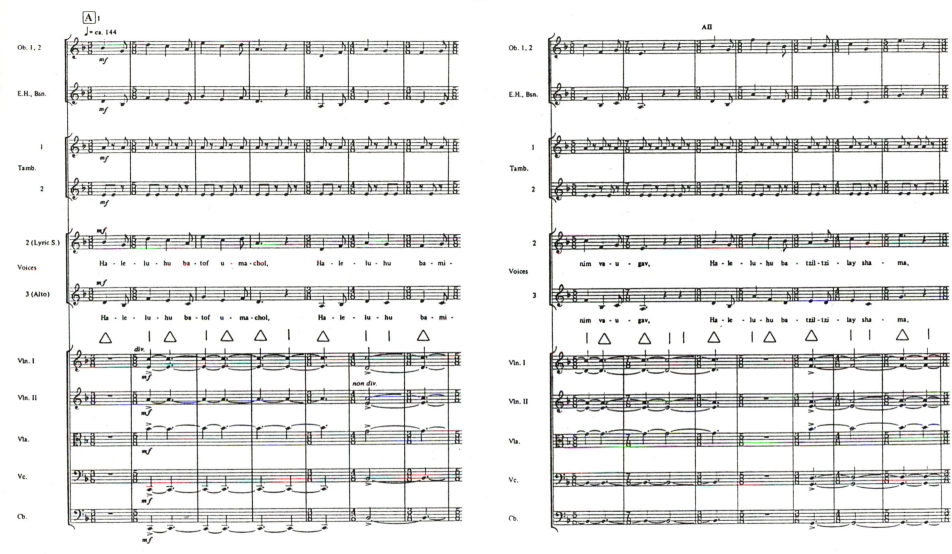

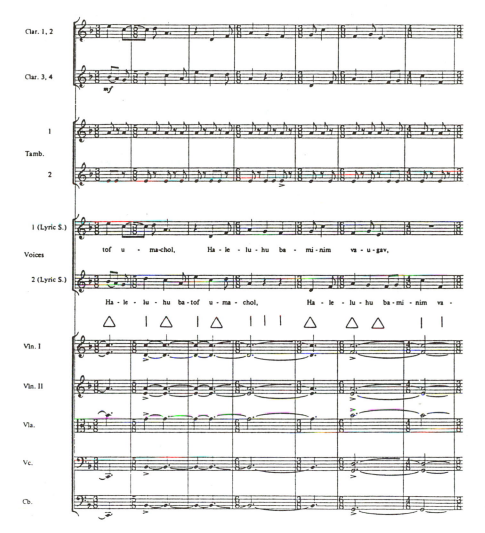

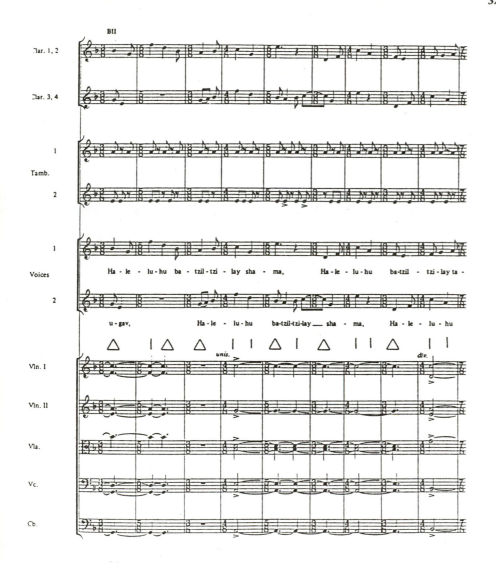

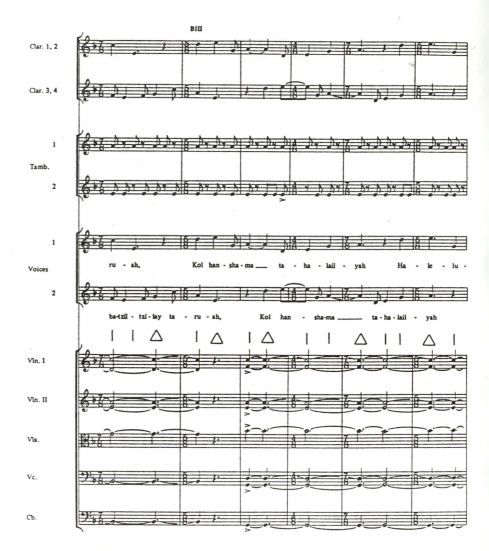

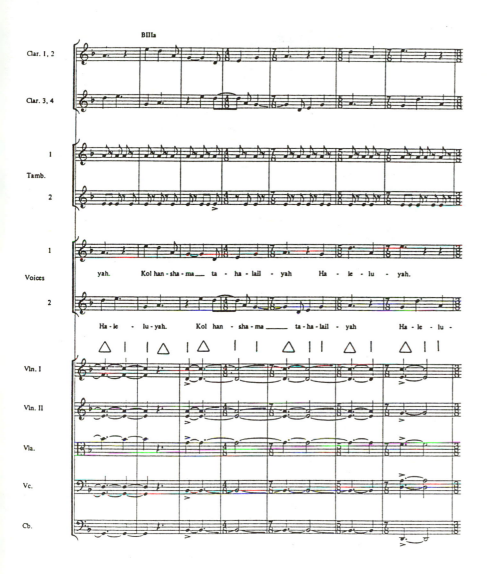

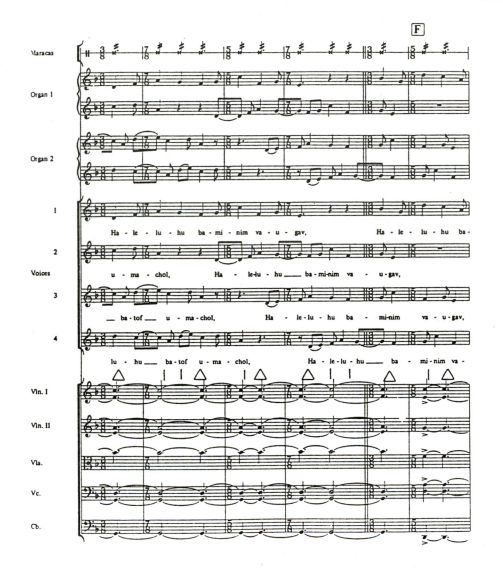

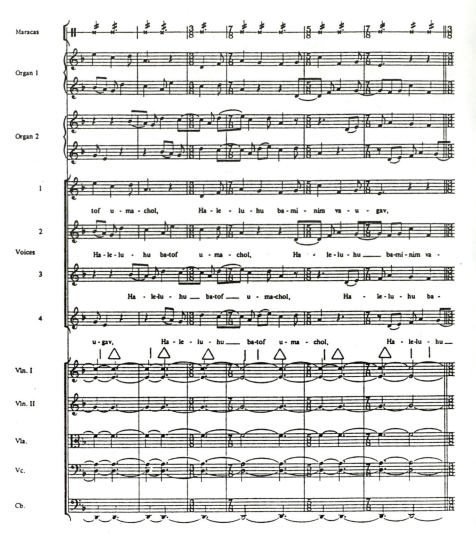

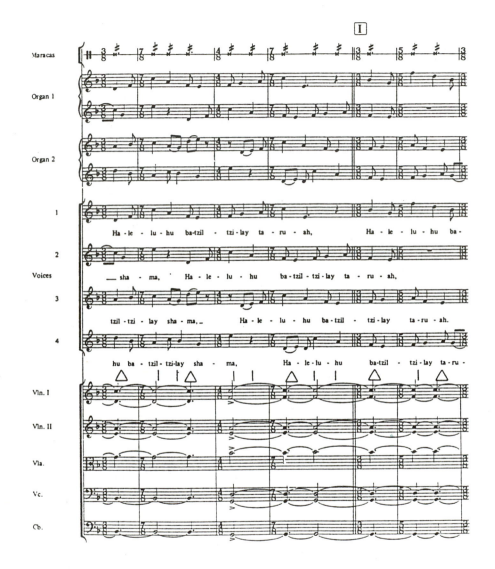

378

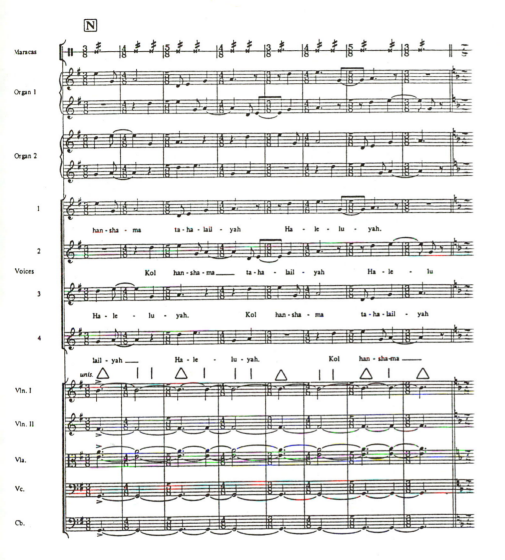

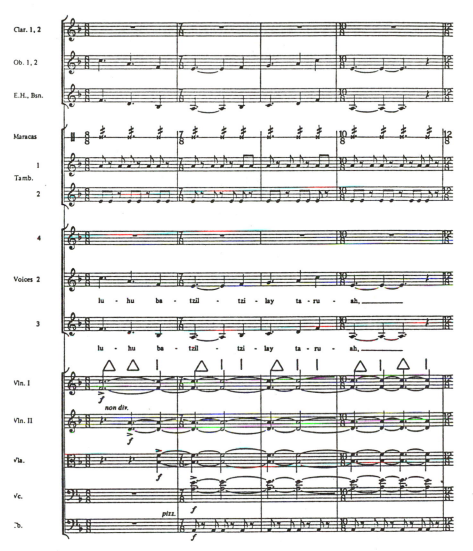

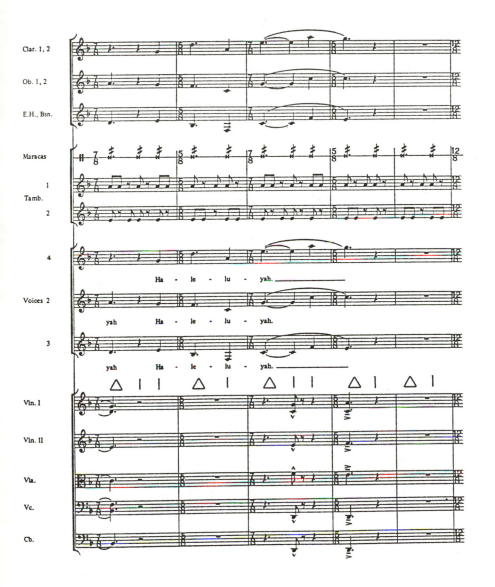
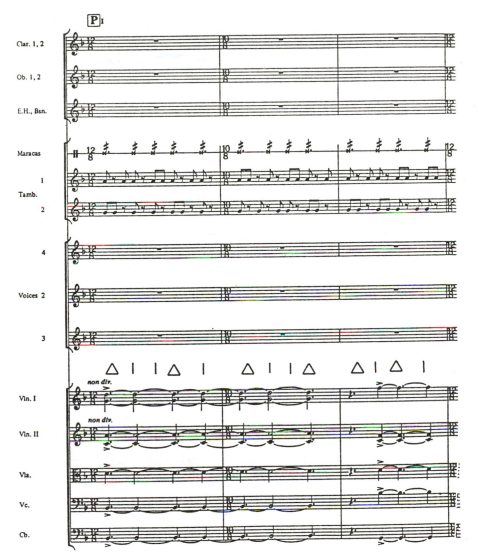

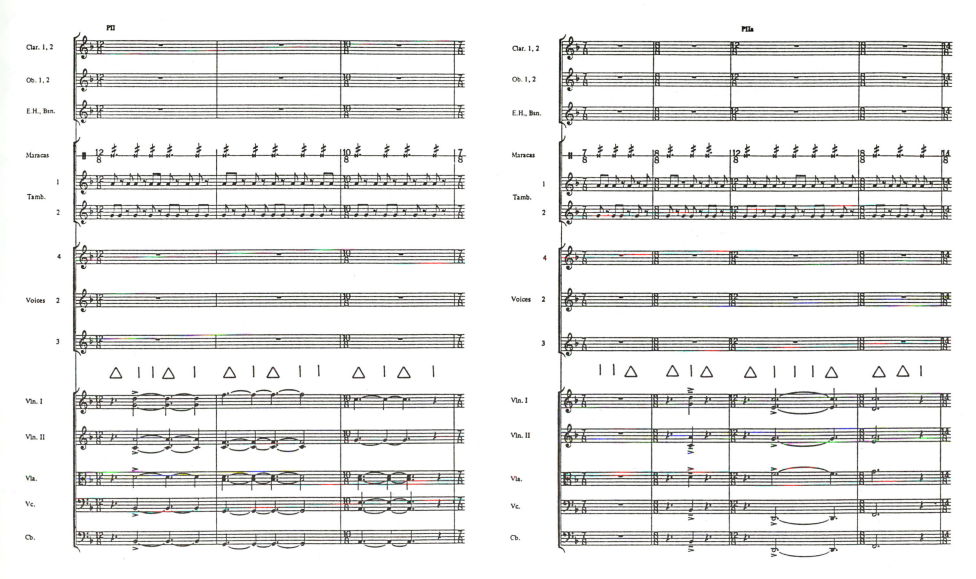

*This movement contains no letter Q.

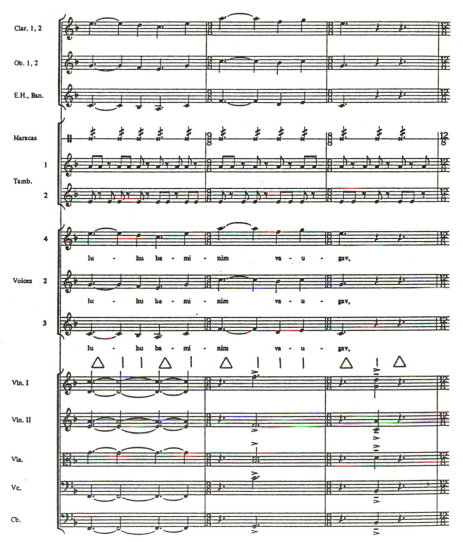

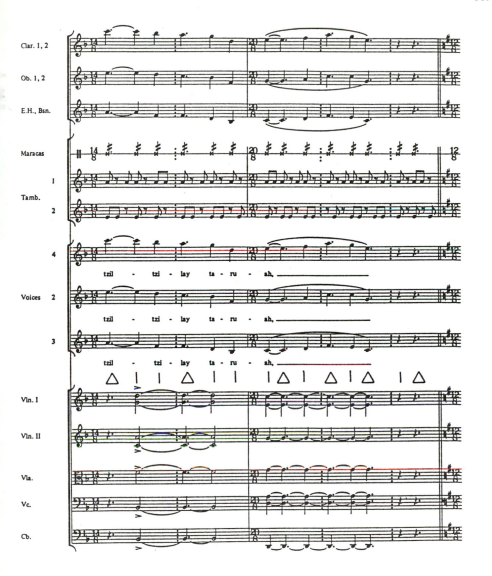

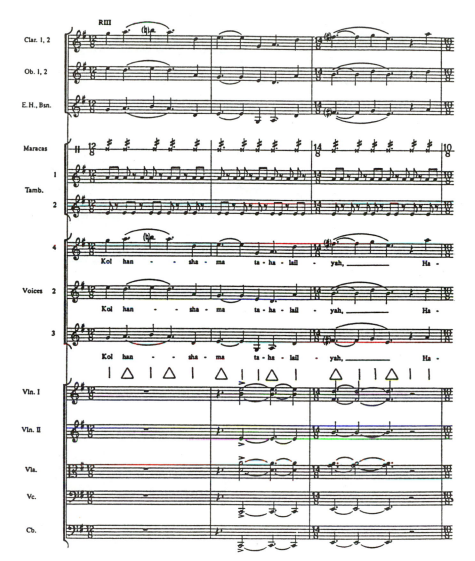

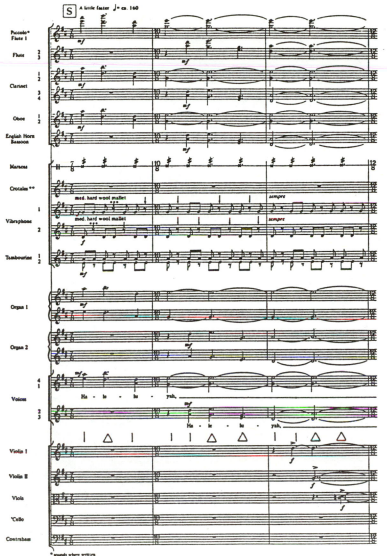

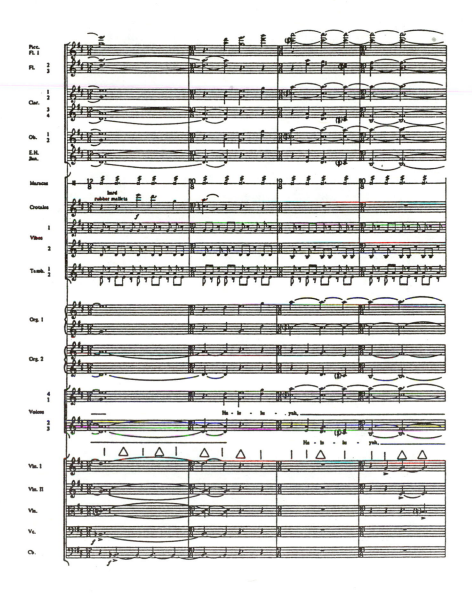

* sounds where written
** sounds an octave higher
*** damp vibraphone note on every rest with hand not holding mallet.

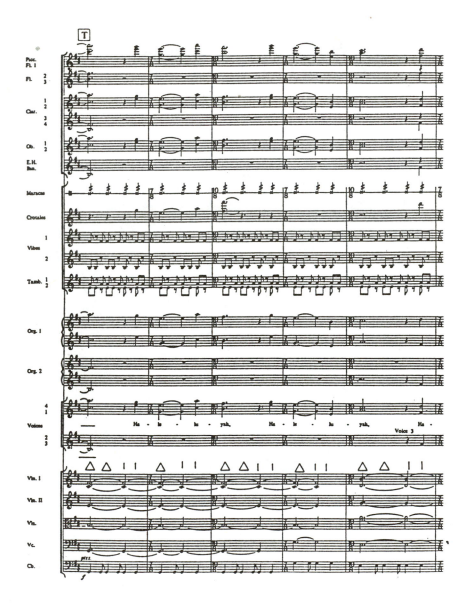

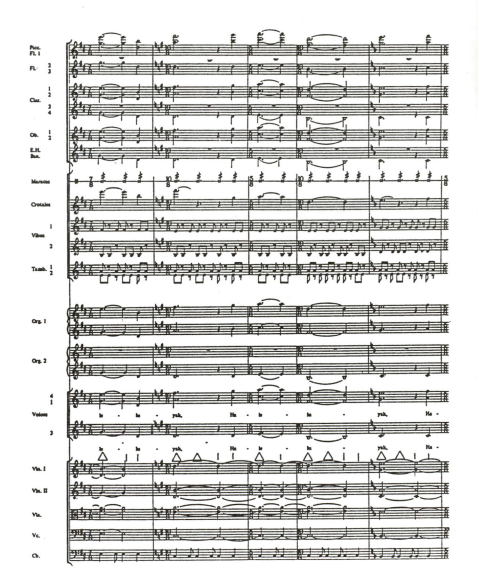

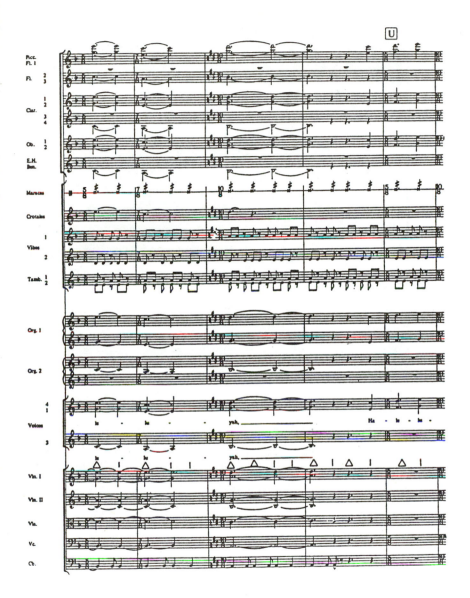
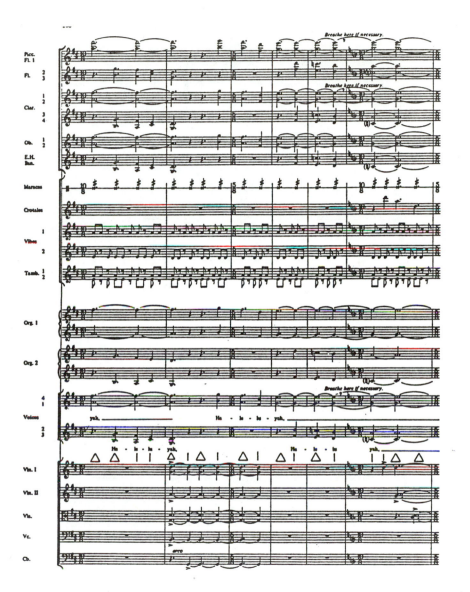

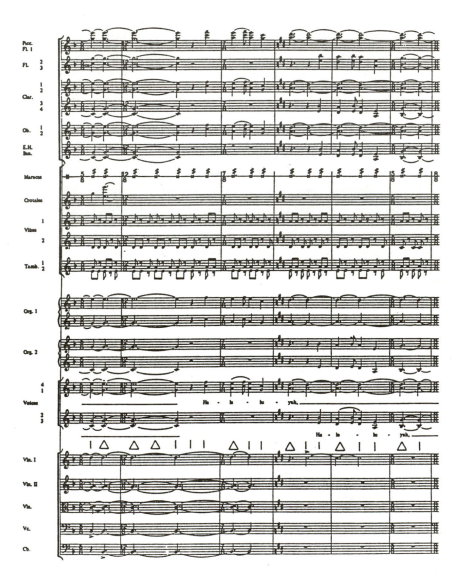
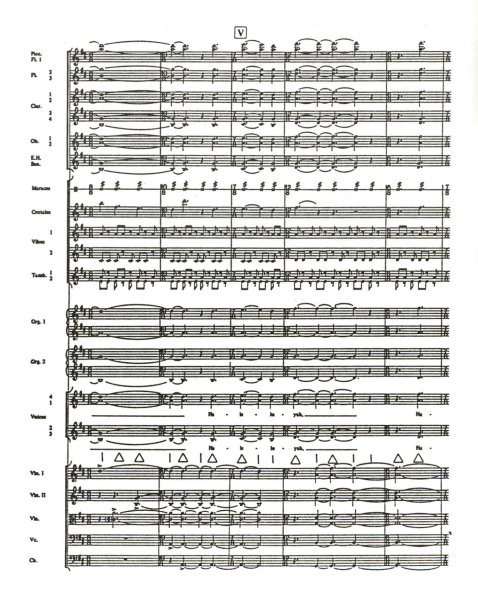

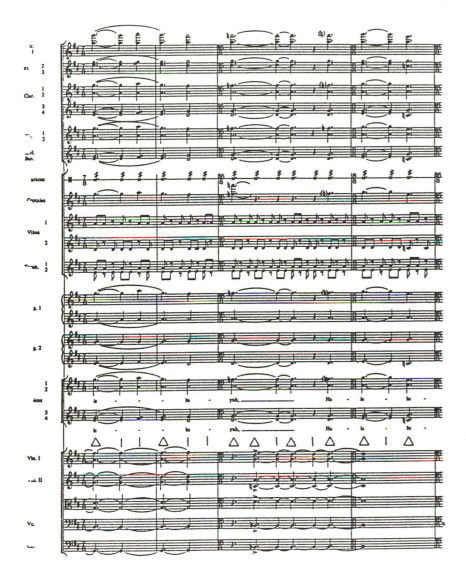

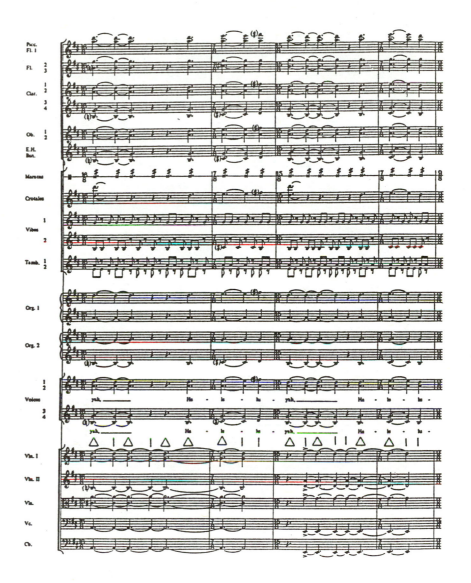

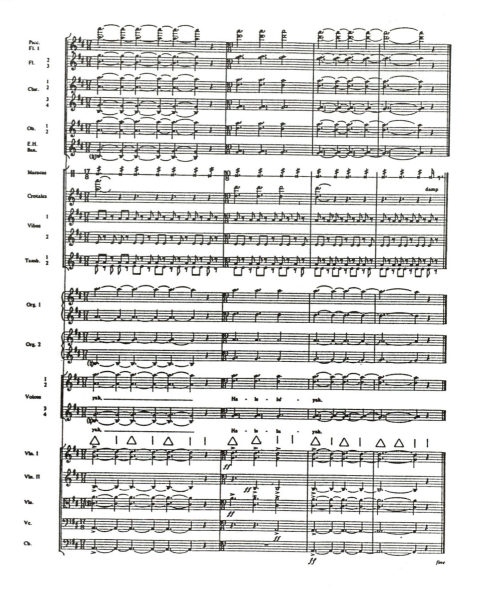

188. CONCERTO GROSSO 1985, mvt. 1
Ellen Taaffe Zwilich (b. 1939)

Appendix A: Names of Instruments and Abbreviations

This table sets forth the English, Italian, German, and French names used in music scores for the various musical instruments, together with their respective abbreviations. Presentation is in the arrangement that has become standard in instrumental scores, reading from the top of the score down: Woodwinds, Brass, Percussion, Strings. Those instruments that are used only occasionally are presented last in this table.

Woodwinds

English	Italian	German	French
Piccolo (Picc.)	Flauto piccolo (Fl. Picc.)	Kleine Flöte (Kl. Fl.)	Petite flûte; Flûte piccolo (Fl. picc.)
Flute (Fl.)	Flauto (Fl.); Flauto grande (Fl. gr.)	Grosse Flöte (Fl. gr.)	Flûte (Fl.)
Alto Flute	Flauto contralto (Fl. c-alto)	Altflöte	Flûte en sol
	[pl., Flauti]	[pl., Flöten]	[pl., Flûtes]
Oboe (Ob.)	Oboe (Ob.)	Hoboe (Hb.); Oboe (Ob.)	Hautbois (Hb.)
	[pl., Oboi]	[pl., Hoboen, Oboen]	[pl., Hautbois]
English Horn (E. H.)	Corno inglese (C.; C.i.; Cor. ingl.)	Englisches Horn (Englh.; E. H.)	Cor anglais (C. A.)
Sopranino Clarinet	Clarinetto piccolo (Cl. picc.; Clar. picc.)		
Clarinet (C.; Cl.; Clt.; Clar.)	Clarinetto (Cl.; Clar.)	Klarinette (Kl.)	Clarinette (Cl.)
	[pl., Clarinetti]	[pl., Klarinetten]	[pl., Clarinettes]
Bass Clarinet (B. Cl.)	Clarinetto basso (Cl. b.; Cl. basso; Clar. basso)	Bassklarinette (Bkl.; Bs. Kl.; B.-Kl.)	Clarinette basse (Cl. bs.)
Bassoon (Bsn.; Bssn.)	Fagotto (Fag.; Fg.)	Fagott (Fag.; Fg.)	Basson (Bssn.)
Contrabassoon (C. Bsn.)	Contrafagotto (Cfg.; C. Fag.; Cont. F.)	Kontrafagott (Kfg.)	Contrebasson (C. bssn.; Cbn.)
	[pl., Fagotti]	[pl., Fagotte]	[pl., Bassons]

Brass

English	Italian	German	French
French Horn, or Horn (Hr.; Hn.)	Corno (Cor.; C.)	Horn (Hr.)	Cor; Cor à piston
	[pl., Corni]	[pl., Hörner (Hrn.)]	[pl., Cors]
Trumpet (Tpt.; Trpt.; Trp.; Tr.)	Tromba (Tr.)	Trompete (Tr.; Trp.)	Trompette (Tr.)
	[pl., Trombe]	[pl., Trompeten]	[pl., Trompettes]
Trombone (Tr.; Tbe.; Trb.; Trbe.; Trm.)	Trombone (Tbn.)	Posaune (Ps.; Pos.)	Trombone (Trb.)
	[pl., Tromboni (Tbni.; Trni.)]	[pl., Posaunen]	[pl., Trombones]
Tuba (Tb.)	Tuba (Tb.; Tba.)	Tuba (Tb.); Basstuba (Btb.)	Tuba (Tb.)

Percussion

English	Italian	German	French
Percussion (Perc.)	Percussione	Schlagzeug (Schlag.)	Batterie (Batt.)
Timpani (Timp.); Kettledrums (K. D.)	Timpani (Timp.; Tp.)	Pauken (Pk.)	Timbales (Timb.)
Snare Drum (S. D.)	Tamburo piccolo (Tamb. picc.); Tamburo militaire	Kleine Trommel (Kl. Tr.)	Caisse Claire (C. cl.); Tambour (Militaire) (Tamb. milit.)
Tenor Drum (T. Dr.)	Cassa Rullante	Wirbeltrommel	Caisse Roulante
Bass Drum (B. Dr.)	Gran Cassa (G. C.; Gr. C.; Gr. Cassa)	Grosse Trommel (Gr. Tr.)	Grosse Caisse (Gr. c.)
Cymbals (Cym.; Cymb.)	Piatti (P.; Ptti.; Piat.)	Becken (Beck.)	Cymbales (Cym.)
Tambourine (Tamb.)	Tamburino (Tamb.)	Schellentrommel; Tambourin (Tamb.)	Tambour de Basque (T. de B.; Tamb. de B.; Tamb. de Basque)
Triangle (Trgl.)	Triangolo (Trgl.)	Triangel	Triangle (Triang.)
Tam-tam; Gong (Tam-T.)	Tam-tam	Tam-tam	Tam-tam
Orchestra Bells; Glockenspiel (Glsp.)	Campanelli (Cmp.)	Glockenspiel (Glsp.)	Jeu de Timbres; Carillon
Tubular Bells; Chimes	Campane (Cmp.)	Glocken	Jeu de Cloches; Cloches
Antique Cymbals; Crotales (Crot.)	Piatti antichi; Crotali	Zimbeln; Antiken Zimbeln	Cymbales Antiques; Crotales
Xylophone (Xyl.)	Xilofono	Xylophon	Xylophone (Xyl.)
Siren			Sirène
Cowbells	Cencerro	Kuhlglocken; Herdenglocken	Sonnailles
Wood Blocks (W. Bl.)	Blocco de Legno Cinese	Holzblock	Bloc de Bois
Castanets	Castagnette	Kastagnetten	Castagnettes

Strings

English	Italian	German	French
Violin (V.; Vln.; Vi.)	Violino (V.; Vl.; Vln.)	Violine (V.; Vl.; Vln.) Geige (Gg.)	Violon (V.; Vl.; Vln.)
Viola (Va.; Vl.) [pl., Vas.]	Viola (Va.; Vla.) [pl., Viole (Vle.)]	Bratsche (Br.)	Alto (A.)
Violoncello; 'Cello (Vcl.; Vc.)	Violoncello (Vc.; Vlc.; Vcllo.)	Violoncell (Vc.; Vlc.)	Violoncelle (Vc.)
Double Bass (D. Bs.)	Contrabasso (Cb.; C.B.) [pl., Contrabassi; Bassi (C. Bassi; Bi.)]	Kontrabass (Kb.)	Contrebasse (C.-B.)

Other Instruments Used Occasionally

When included in the orchestra, notation for these instruments is usually placed in the score between percussion and strings.

English	Italian	German	French
Harp (Hp.; Hrp.)	Arpa (A.; Arp.)	Harfe (Hrf.)	Harpe (Hp.)
Piano (Pno.)	Pianoforte (P-f.; Pft.)	Klavier (Kl.)	Piano
Celeste (Cel.)	Celesta	Celesta	Célesta
Harpsichord	Cembalo	Cembalo	Clavecin
Organ (Org.)	Organo	Orgel	Orgue

Appendix B: Some Technical Terms
Frequently Used in Orchestral Scores

English	Italian	German	French
Muted; With mute(s)	Con sordino	mit Dämpfer; Gedämpft (for horns)	Sourdine(s)
Take off mutes	Via sordini	Dämpfer(n) Weg	Enlevez les sourdines
Without mute	Senza sordino	Ohne Dämpfer	Sans sourdine
Divided	Divisi (div.)	Geteilt (get.)	Divisé(e)s (div.)
Divided in 3 parts (or whatever number is specified)	div. a 3	Dreifach	div. à 3
In unison (unis.)	Unisono (unis.)	Zusammen	Unis
Solo	Solo	Allein	Seul
All	Tutti	Alle	Tous
(First player only) 1.	1°	1ste; einfach	1er
1., 2. (first and second players on separate parts)	1°, 2°	1ste, 2te	1er, 2e
a2 (2 players on same part)	a2	zu 2	à 2
Near the bridge	Sul ponticello	am Steg	Sur le chevalet
Bow over the fingerboard	Sul tastiera; Sul tasto	am Griffbrett	sur la touche
With the wood of the bow	Col legno	mit Holz; col Legno	Avec le bois
At the point of the bow	Punta d'arco	Spitze	Pointe; de la pointe
At the frog of the bow	al Tallone	am Frosch	du talon
Half (half of a string section is to play)	la metà	die Hälfte	la moitié
Stopped (horns)	Chiuso; chiusi	Gestopft	Bouché; bouchés
Open	Aperto; aperti	Offen	Ouvert
With soft stick; with soft mallet	Bacchetta di spugna	mit Schwammschlegel	Baguette d'éponge; baguette molle
With hard stick(s)	Bacchette di legno	mit Holzschlegeln	Baguette(s) en bois
(Directive to change tuning, or instrument):			
Change C to E	Sol Muta in Mi	C nach E umstimmen	Changez Do en Mi
Change to piccolo (or whatever instr.)	Muta in Piccolo	Piccolo nehmen	Changez en piccolo
Stand, or Desk	Leggio	Pult	Pupitre
Ordinary; In ordinary way (play in ordinary manner, after having played sul ponticello, for example)	Modo ordinario	Gewöhnlich	Mode ordinaire; position nat.

Index